SIT in the SUN

SIT in the SUN

And Other Lessons in the Spiritual Wisdom of Cats

Jon M. Sweeney

Broadleaf Books
Minneapolis

SIT IN THE SUN

And Other Lessons in the Spiritual Wisdom of Cats

Cover design: 1517 Media

Cover and interior illustrations by Jennifer Khatun

Print ISBN: 978-1-5064-8227-9

eBook ISBN: 978-1-5064-8228-6

For Boots, Spike, Cleo, Cortez, Bowie-hena,
Katana, Mia, Martin, and Rosa

CONTENTS

PREFACE 1

CHAPTER ONE   Surrender to Relax 9

CHAPTER TWO   Find the Love inside You . . . 21

CHAPTER THREE   Be Aware of the Love
around You 33

CHAPTER FOUR   Play Joyfully 45

CHAPTER FIVE   Eat Regularly and Well . . . 59

CHAPTER SIX   Sit in the Sun 69

CHAPTER SEVEN   Voice Your Opinion 77

CHAPTER EIGHT   Keep to a Schedule 87

CHAPTER NINE   Wake Up 97

CHAPTER TEN   Sit Your Ground 105

CONTENTS

CHAPTER ELEVEN — Refuse to Be Tamed. 113

CHAPTER TWELVE — Don't Take Embarrassment Seriously 127

CHAPTER THIRTEEN — See into Things. 139

CHAPTER FOURTEEN — Know That You Are Loved. 149

CHAPTER FIFTEEN — Be Persistent and Thankful 161

CHAPTER SIXTEEN — Quiet Yourself 171

CHAPTER SEVENTEEN — Pounce Frequently. 179

EPILOGUE — Caution and Promise. . . 187

SOURCES AND FURTHER READING. 193

ABOUT THE AUTHOR 199

ACKNOWLEDGMENTS 201

NOTES. 203

PREFACE

I have lived with birds, fish, rodents, dogs, amphibians, and bugs, but no species has been as uniformly delightful and spiritually informative in my life as the cats with whom I have shared so much. No other species has taught and inspired me as much as the cat. I realize that I am in a big club, and I thank you for joining me to pursue what this means.

There are also others in the club you are joining, people from the pages of history, including political leaders too, who have loved and spent their lives with cats, notably the US president Abraham Lincoln and the British prime minister who saved his nation from Hitler, Winston Churchill. Other interesting writer and artist companions of felines have included Ernest Hemingway, Alice Walker, Margaret Atwood, Pablo Picasso, and Georgia O'Keeffe. Some I'll quote and refer to in the chapters to come. Many of them understood the spiritual wisdom of cats.

I hope that you've come to this book because there's a cat in your life you love. And assuming that you have, I am going to also assume that we are all here for other reasons as well, among them, because we sense a stirring in our souls that tells us the meaning of life is not fully explained by biology, environment, or luck. There is something else going on in the world. There is something we understand as ultimately mysterious and indefinable. As a friend of mine who worked at Fermi Labs outside Chicago used to put it: "Let's boil it down to this: If you could take all the atoms out of the universe, I believe there would be something left." We are not altogether explained by our bodies, our surroundings, or even the atoms in the universe. There is something more. In fact, for some of us, that may even be a name for God: *Something More.*

Then, there is probably another reason. We know that the stirring in our souls is not simply a feeling inside. So much that stirs our souls and waters our spirits is what we experience through our senses. It is what touches our skin, looks into our eyes, tingles our tongues, leads our noses, and makes noises that our ears take in all day long—that which comes through the created world surrounding us, of which we are only a very small part; all of it is essential to our spirituality. Most immediately, this surrounding world comes to us through the creatures that live in our homes. We have welcomed them in because we like how they stir us up and inspire us.

I believe that a relationship with an animal is a part of our unfolding as human beings. There is a revealing and opening of ourselves as people that takes places in close connection to other species. They show us our animal side. They reveal the world to us in ways that books, and even other people, cannot. Sometimes, ironically, it's the animal that even reveals our humanity to us. They help us discover our senses, responses, and feelings in ways that other humans cannot as much. If you have loved an animal, you have probably experienced this. You know what I am talking about.

A spiritual dimension of life unfolds in a relationship between a human and another animal species. We begin to grasp our soul's capacities, living with cats, in ways that human-to-human connections cannot as fully do. There is another mind and heart and spirit (yes, animals have spirits) at play around us, and we begin to unfold as we discover how and why we are different from these others.

It is from my cats that I have learned much, which is not why you are here, but it is why I am. And because I learn and understand best when I write, I wanted to put down on paper some of these lessons—and because they have changed my life.

To look upon an animal companion with an intention to find similarities of spirit and heart is to begin to know ourselves in an expanded way, but then to look upon an animal companion with a gaze of love, already grasping a shared understanding, brings something particularly special. If you haven't experienced this already, I hope this book will accompany that experience for you.

The father of four children, I love them all, but my youngest, who is wicked smart and tends to lack sentimentality, at age eight expressed the ambivalence of human love very precociously. While walking home from school, she said to me, "I would declare you the greatest dad in the world except that I've never had another dad and so I really don't know." That sort of ambiguity doesn't come with a beloved animal. Unless the human screws it up, the animal's devotion tends to be total and unquestioning—and I admit to liking that quality of the relationship quite a lot.

I have lived with nine cats so far in my life. Boots was my cat when I was little. My brother and I used to dress her in our underwear, until one day when Boots ran away. I don't blame her. Seventeen years later, three kittens were abandoned on my doorstep in 1989 when I was still young and first married. They filled my first decade of adult life. Several years later, I adopted two fully grown cats when a colleague was moving away and couldn't take them with him out of state. I refer to them as my Jewish cats because they came with Hebrew names. (More on that later.) My friend was Jewish and had attended cantorial school. Next, a couple years after their arrival, when my young son was having trouble handling and expressing his anger, a wise pediatrician recommended an animal companion for him, so we found Joe a kitten of his own. I share stories about these cats in the pages that follow. Most of all, though, I tell of the two kittens—now cats—we adopted in late April

2020. Before they came to us, their human foster mother named them Martin and Rosa, after Martin Luther King Jr. and Rosa Parks, because they were born in February—Black History Month.

As you read the book you may think, at times, I presume to understand them too much. No doubt, I am guilty of this related to cats, and in almost any aspect of my life. Other times you may also think I impart feelings in my cats that they cannot possibly experience. Maybe so, but while Martin and Rosa cannot speak a language I understand, we do share ways of communicating. And I'm happy to believe that I mean so much to them. And every indication offers the same on their part.

There is another way in which I appreciate cats that is similar to what I appreciate in other nonhuman species. The dogs in my house and the birds in my woods have taught me this too: namely, in the words of philosopher John Gray, "Cats do not need to examine their lives, because they do not doubt that life is worth living." This is why I could also be accused of wanting to be around humans less often, and cats more often, the older I become. And to learn that sense of worthwhile life from them. They do not doubt.

They do not wonder what it all means. They have their own storylines going, but they don't get up in the middle of the night to worry about the details. My cats have always—like great trees, but even better, because you can hear their purring—offered a kind of steadiness and presence without a lot of talk.

Jon M. Sweeney
October 29, 2022
National Cat Day in the United States

CHAPTER ONE

Surrender to Relax

I have attended thousands of religious services,
maybe a hundred spiritual retreats. But in all my years, I
don't think I have ever heard a homily or Dvar Torah or
dharma talk on the subject of relaxation. Our teachers rarely
help us incorporate relaxation into our lives, let alone our
spiritual practices.

It may simply be the language used to describe its practice that is different. Lately, I have been discovering ways to
relax that fit my practice, and I have been finding teachings
about this in a variety of religious traditions and contexts.
One of the most profound of these has been on *surrender*. And surrender, I now realize, can be a synonym for
relaxation when a spiritual vocabulary is overlaid with our
everyday vocabulary. When a spiritual teacher guides me to
surrender, it can be very similar to what my mother meant

when she was trying to tell me how to settle down and relax. I was not good at it then, and I am often not good at it now. So, I am thankful for this new teacher—I will get to him in a moment—but this is a lesson I have learned from my two cats as well.

It is often said that when the student is ready, the teacher appears. And sometimes the teacher is not whom or what you expect. It's also become clear to me recently how much I can learn from ordinary, domestic, nonreligious experiences. My friend Ronald Rolheiser once pointed to this lesson in an experience from the life of the hermit and mystic Carlo Carretto. As Rolheiser explained it:

> A much respected spiritual mentor, [Carretto] had spent most of his life living by himself as a hermit in the Sahara desert, praying in silence and translating scripture into the Bedouin language. On one of his visits home to Italy, sitting with his mother, he was struck by the fact that she, an earthy practical woman who had raised a large family and who had gone through whole years of

her life so preoccupied with the duties of raising her children that she never had any quality time alone, was more of a contemplative than he was, her hermit son, who had spent years alone in solitude trying to block out the distractions of the world so as to pray.

It wasn't hermit life in the Sahara that taught Carretto contemplation so much as watching his mother at home.

There are many other, more ordinary, examples of this lesson—that the ordinary and the domestic, even the mundane—can be our most profound teachers. I have good friends who for decades claimed one of their most important spiritual practices was scooping the poop of their fostered cats. What better way to learn humility? Carlo Carretto realized that his mother had become a great contemplative by raising a brood of children and finding the quiet within; how better to become the humblest person on the block than by scooping a busy cat box with joy or corralling and nurturing young children while remaining free every day of your life?

Also recently, I read an interesting new book by an atheist preparing to become a chaplain about how she was learning to pray and do other spiritual practices by reading novels such as *Jane Eyre* and *The Great Gatsby*. I suspect that we will identify many more ways in which the domestic informs us spiritually, even religiously, in the years ahead. For now, and for me, it's the cats in my house.

I'm a spiritual pilgrim. I've practiced with teachers of many different traditions and paths. With roots in my own religious tradition—Catholicism, with a monastic emphasis—I continue to look for wisdom, beauty, and truth wherever it can be found. And this past year I have found myself learning most of all from my cats. Maybe you have experienced that too.

My at-home spiritual wise ones—Martin and Rosa—are siblings. They were born early in February 2020. Their human foster mother named them and cared for them from just after birth. When they were seven weeks old, we adopted them, in late April, when they each reached two pounds.

They are my teachers today. They embody lessons in great spiritual practices that resonate with me. I watch and learn from them in the way that someone might watch and learn from a guru, by living together side by side.

In many spiritual traditions, there is a saying that varies only in the details. It goes something like this: What did you learn from sitting at the feet of the Buddha (or the Zen master, the rabbi, the guru, etc.)? I learned how to tie my shoes (or how to stack wood, how to open doors quietly, etc.). We learn more from accompanying a spiritual teacher than from taking notes as she lectures. I sit with Martin and Rosa, listen to them, and even seek to imitate them in at least seventeen identifiable ways. They have much to teach me, and I have much to learn. We all do, from our cat teachers.

Sufi sheiks remind us that the only way to truly know the love of God is to surrender to God. This means causing the selfish urgings inside of us to slow down and perhaps cease altogether. This sort of surrender is an act of the will and the heart. We surrender our ego, our thoughts of being in charge of our lives, so that God may fill us more completely. Sufis thus discover the spiritual lesson of learning to "die before you die," as well as the blessings that come from this discovery. And when they learn the practice well, they also learn how to relax. The two go hand in hand.

In my own Christian tradition, these teachings on surrender have influenced how I pray. I have almost completely abandoned the form of prayer that asks God for things and tells God what I need or want. Instead, prayer has taken on contemplative purposes in my life; it is an exercise in ego abandonment.

As long as our ego and our will are permitted to rule us, we will experience spiritual discomfort. For this reason, the great Persian Sufi poet Hafiz once said to himself, "You are your own veil, Hafiz. Get out of the way." Similar teaching appears in other religious traditions. The great rabbi of the Civil Rights Era in the United States, Abraham Joshua Heschel, for instance, said: "The greatest beauty grows at the greatest distance from the ego."

When we discover why and how to surrender to the Divine, a sort of calmness begins to override anxiety. As the calm enters, we realize those selfish urges of ours (perhaps of appetite or for sex, acquiring unnecessary things, frivolity, or actions that ultimately harm someone) not only do us and others no good, but they keep us on edge, unable to relax.

The Sufi teacher from whom I've been learning to surrender, Sufi sheik Ihsan Alexander, offers a way into Sufi meditation through relaxation, which I've found to be a beautiful and simple practice. Ihsan, who lives in Southern California, has taught this method to many people from all walks of life, including for instance members of the US Marine Corps, who have an urgent need to be able to decompress before and after stressful situations.

Not only do we realize in meditation—whether this type or some other—that our appetites are not helping us, we also see how appetites, and most every form of passion, rarely provide us a way to God. There is running toward God, following our passions (which are similar to appetites) in pursuit of the Holy, and occasionally that's productive. But then there is also letting the passions fall away, like leaves from trees in autumn, or the parachute-like pappi that you gently blow from a dandelion in late summer. Letting go is far better and more productive.

When I meditate to surrender in the way that Sheik Ihsan teaches, and when I relax on my way to God, I recognize that my cats have been there long before me. They seem to intuitively know how to surrender.

Take a moment to remember how your felines look before and after they have surrendered. Before, there is anxiety, pleading looks, and sometimes urgent or aggressive behavior. After, there is yawning, stretching, lying about like well-fed big cats in the wild. They are just like human beings—they are like us—for whom basic needs must first be met.

My Rosa is black and white. She looks at me earnestly in the morning when she is telling me that she is very hungry. Her long neck sticks far out beyond her front paws, as if she is leaning into the look that she is giving me in these moments. I may have been making coffee, drinking coffee, reading, praying, and walking back and forth in the house without paying attention to anyone but myself before Rosa gives me this look. When I see her, I'm immediately reminded that it is our responsibility to care for each other. It is my responsibility to feed Rosa and Martin so that their most basic, healthy appetites are satisfied. The "look" from Rosa is a reminder of our shared creatureliness and need to care for one another.

Then, there is Martin. He is no less earnest in his desire to get my attention when hungry. In fact, he's the one who will do more than give a withering glance. Martin will walk across my key-tapping fingers and perhaps nibble my ankles until I pay him the proper attention. He cannot be ignored. But this is good, and as it should be. He knows his need for food, attention, love.

Then, once his basic needs have been met, Martin will sometimes lie back in my arm, cradled like an infant. Breakfast is over. His body, his eyes, his paws are all at peace and relaxed. You've likely witnessed the beautiful moments after feeding a cat when they may like to cuddle or be near you. It feels like a blessing and a prayer: May we all feel this comfortable and relaxed at least sometimes in our lives.

Christian mystical teacher Cynthia Bourgeault, a faculty member at the Center for Action and Contemplation in New Mexico, echoes these lessons of relaxation and surrender in her work. She teaches that it is when we are able to go deeply to our core and relax and let go of our appetites that we find God's love waiting there for us. Craving, wanting, and needing stand in the way and are "on the surface" of ourselves. Love is deeper in. But we can access it. In her recent book, *Eye of the Heart*, she explains: "As soon as one relaxes spatially and allows the larger picture to fill in, suddenly the mercy reappears, like the full moon from behind the darkened clouds."

How often do we allow ourselves to relax spatially—where we live, where we are? How often do we go through a whole day like a moon that remains hidden behind dark clouds? It is lonely out there. And I see the household cats reading me, telling me to relax.

Let me add that I often don't close my eyes in meditation. I keep them open. And I sometimes watch Martin and Rosa relax into surrender as my own way of going to that place. In this way, my cats truly are my spiritual guides and might be good guides for us all as we try to imbibe in ourselves what felines already seem to understand so well.

They will relax-surrender in the middle of the floor, even in the busiest hallway in our home, even as I nearly stumble on them or try to walk past them in a rush—since I'm too often moving quickly from one thing to another—I think, *Move!* until I remember: they are surrendering. They are experiencing a kind of relaxation that reminds me I want to recognize that in myself as well. They have given themselves over to something much larger than themselves. Cats seem to recognize, with their lives, that they are small creatures, and they continue to remind us we are invited to do the same.

A (Sometimes Cat, Sometimes Human) Spiritual Practice

You might wish to find Ihsan Alexander's "Relax in Divine Surrender" meditation on the web at the link below. The teaching is about twenty minutes long. I encourage you to sit with him (and perhaps be in the good company of your cat companion who knows some of this wisdom already) and try the practice, then to try it again, and perhaps make it a part of your regular practice too. https:// insighttimer.com/ihsanalexander/guided-meditations/ relax-in-divine-surrender

CHAPTER TWO

Find the Love inside You

I know there are those who say cats are selfish. I have heard this all my life, particularly from friends who feel that loyalty to their dog is somehow enhanced by criticizing cats. But I don't think it is possible to find cats selfish if you have ever in fact lived with one, or frankly, if you've simply paid close attention to them.

Even academic research has shown that it isn't true that cats are selfish. Animal behavior scientists, in a 2017 study summarized for the scholarly journal *Behavioral Processes*, showed how domestic cats tend to prefer human contact and interaction more than they prefer food and playing with toys. Two years later, another study in the same journal found that, in the language of the article's abstract, "Cats are facultatively social animals." That's academese for saying, cats tend to decide to be sociable. And, the researchers found, cats use their sociability faculties almost in direct proportion to the sociability and love that they receive from their humans. That sounds a lot like human relational and behavior patterns as well.

Another myth follows the first and is also important to dispel: Even if we recognize that cats enjoy being around us, and with us, it is still commonplace to assume that they are doing so only to get something selfish out of the interaction. "She only wants to be fed," we say, or, "He just wants attention."

Even contemporary literature offers up examples of this assumption. Take the speculative fiction writer, Ursula Le Guin, who wrote a late-career novella in the voice of a cat named Pard. It's a funny book in which, at one point, Le Guin has Pard saying of the human who cares for him, "What I like to use about her is the place behind her knees on the bed, and the top of her head, which having a kind of fur reminds me a little of my Mother, so sometimes I get on the pillow with it and knead it. This works best when she is asleep." The humor comes in the cat saying, "What

I like to use about her . . . ," as if that's all there is to the relationship. Is our cats' love for us completely summarized in these sorts of ways, as selfish and self-interested? That's not all of it.

Most house cats who grew up in loving care are affectionate in one way or another. In fact, one plausible theory of purring is that it originates in the memories of their mother's heartbeat, and when they reproduce that sound for you, it is as a sign of gratefulness and love. Purring can first be heard in nursing kittens at about one week of age, and it seems to indicate an "all is well" contentedness, or more specifically, that the milk is being received just fine. So, when a cat proves to be aloof, it is probably best explained by personality, trauma, the feral cat fighting for survival, rather than as selfishness. As to personality, there are as many cat personalities as there are cats. You'll find introverted cats and extroverted cats. You've likely been around cats you'd label as thinking cats or feeling cats. (Someday, maybe I will work up Enneagram types for them as well.) Just as we would not call an introverted human being selfish, who needs more downtime, more alone time, why would we label an introverted cat with only one checked box: selfish cat? Some cats are predisposed to spend more time alone.

Rosa is an introvert. Every cat is, in some respects, an introvert. We know that they often don't like to be looked at for too long, or at least, to be stared at. To a cat, staring is what you do at prey. This is why cat-savvy humans meeting a cat for the first time will warm up to a cat using nonchalant means to attract the cat's attention. When visiting a friend with a cat and she wanders into the room for the first time, usually from along a wall, or rubbing against a piece of furniture, because that's what introverts do, I don't look directly at her. I look away slightly, and if I'm sitting in a chair, I lay one hand down at my side near the floor in the hope and expectation that she might come over to say hello. With the invitation open and the pressure off, she often does.

But there are some more intrepid felines who lean toward a more extroverted lifestyle. Martin most definitely is one of these. When there are strangers in the house, and Rosa is nowhere to be found, Martin is soon walking into the middle of the room heading straight toward the stranger. This is his house, and he'll say hello to whomever he pleases.

But all cats, in my experience, have to learn how to feel comfortable, as places of love, in their own bodies. The outward-turning versus inward-turning of the extrovert-introvert scale has little to do with this; this is about immature cats becoming mature ones—just as human beings have to learn these things. Everyone has seen, at one time or another, a cat cleaning themselves. This is perhaps the most universal bit of feline knowledge that human beings possess: Cats are clean, very clean. Well, this in fact serves several purposes, among them something that healthy cats do to process their feelings as they learn to be comfortable in themselves.

Throughout history we have a record of human beings who are unable to understand this. In medieval Europe, for instance, this self-cleaning by cats wasn't viewed positively. Because cats clean themselves, including their orifices, medieval people found this distasteful to the point that they used it as an analogy to express anger with religious leaders. For instance, if it was revealed their bishop had committed sexual sin or perversion, they would draw the medieval version of cartoons in the margins of manuscripts, showing human lechers attempting to "clean" themselves up, like cats do.

Today we have a much more positive view of cat self-care and of the value of cleaning ourselves in every method and in every region. (Our analogies have changed, but our view of clergy sin and crime hasn't, nor should it.)

When you watch cats clean themselves, you witness the meditative: They clean thoughtfully, deliberately, mindfully, at stressful moments and also as a regular practice.

Their humans can learn from this example. If we could all pause and care for ourselves with regularity and thoughtfulness, the whole world might reverberate with purrs of love. Loving oneself can be the most difficult practice of all. The great Vietnamese Buddhist monk Thich Nhat Hanh taught that love is an energy that transforms the world. This is the best place to begin. We might even see it in our cats—when we see them grooming, hear them purring, we somehow soften within, and the household has a little more purr-motor to it. As Thay (as his students called him) would say, love must begin inside us. In a book from 2009, *Answers from the Heart*, he explains:

The teaching of the Buddha aims at helping us to generate the energy of love and understanding. If we can practice that energy, it will first of all help us to satisfy our need to be loved. And then, with that capacity of love and understanding, we can embrace the people who are with us now. We can make them happy while we are happy ourselves.

Thay taught that we all have this energy available to us, but obstacles stand in the way of our accessing and expressing it. Remembering the pain of previous relationships is likely our chief obstacle. As Thay would say, you can't ever push those negative experiences and feelings away. They will not simply "go." You have to instead embrace them, accept them as real, so that you might then repair the wound, grow around it, and return to the place where the energy inside of you is love.

Some people do this work in silent, sitting meditation. For me, it's the sounds of purrs or even hisses in myself, where sounding it out loud works much better. Admitting to myself in my own voice, "I am hurt. They hurt me," but then also, "I am more than this pain and this hurt. I want to get better. I want to start again" is helpful. When I say things like this to myself, sometimes over and over, and sometimes loudly, it is kind of like purring for another purpose. I am allowing the noise of what is painful to move from inside my body to outside my body. This practice carries the hope that those lousy feelings may be replaced by loving ones, again, as love fills the empty spaces. It works.

Maybe cats don't go through such a self-conscious process of healing, but I also know that they do not purr all the time. If someone were to purr all the time, we would know that their purring probably comes from an inauthentic place. Or they're faking it. We have all met people who smile easily and say things like, "I love everyone," or suggest they have their spiritual practice together, which leaves us suspecting that perhaps they have become disconnected from real loving, real practice. Like our cats, our true purring arises naturally and effortlessly from inside us as human beings, where there is love in there that's ready to reverberate, and that is the place of love, the place of God.

Pierre Teilhard de Chardin, a Jesuit mystic and paleontologist of the last century, viewed the world through the lens of its raw basic parts—because he studied fossils—as well as through the lens of its essentially mystical unity. In a book called *Human Energy*, he wrote, "Love is the most universal, the most tremendous, and the most mysterious of the cosmic forces." It is this love that brought the universe into being, and it is this same love that continues to hold it together in big and small ways.

No, cats don't hold the universe together—but their purring is like the roar of the oceans or the hum of the earth that cannot quite be heard with the human ear. Their sounds gather together with sounds primeval, natural, and holy. Like the person in meditation who chants "Om," the sacred symbol and sound in Indian religions, meaning ultimate reality itself, and also the soul. A beautiful Mary Oliver poem titled "On the Beach" ends with the poet seeing sunshine at dawn pour itself over small stones near the water and reflecting how that same sun also "shed its light on me, / my own body that loves," reminding her that our human loving is a participation in a much greater loving of which we are a small but essential part. These are not images of sound, but they are also not quiet. Like purring.

Martin and Rosa sometimes embrace in ways that suddenly turn into wrestling that then turn into biting, and I sometimes hear one of them call out as if in pain. Our purring is not a permanent condition. But it helps to know our purring and to find ways to return to it quickly and more often. It can change our world.

Love is the most basic element of life. Before anything else, there was love, and that same love lives in us. If we could only locate it, know it, and express it better in our bodies, I think it would be the start of revealing it more easily to those around us.

A Cat Practice

Purr. Yes, purr. Find a quiet place alone, where you can feel in yourself, and be by yourself, and just purr. No one needs to see you try this (though I expect your cats would not mind at all—I sometimes replay a short audio clip for Martin of his purring), but try it. Listen to the sound that you make and begin to try to hear it as the sound of what is holy inside of you. You may be surprised how this sound reverberates in your body—a new way of praying—making you realize your connectedness with the divine.

CHAPTER THREE

Be Aware of the Love around You

Our cats look to us to love them like a mother, and why shouldn't they? I pet Rosa sometimes in ways that deliberately resemble what a mother cat will do with her kittens. My fingers pull gently on her ears, as I've seen mother cats do with their litter, pulling gently on kitten ears with their tongue. I'll then add distinctive human touches, such as tummy rubbing and, for Rosa especially, gently cupping my whole palm over her eyes, forehead, whiskers, and ears. She loves this. She bows her head and purrs. I hold her in this way only for a few seconds. (Longer than that and I think it goes from comforting to claustrophobic real fast.)

Over time I've learned how to do this, observing what Rosa likes and doesn't. And I imagine that her mother held her tightly in similar ways, otherwise I expect Rosa wouldn't enjoy it so much now.

When I was six, seven, and eight years old, my own mother would place my head on her lap and stroke my hair for twenty minutes or longer while we were in the living room as a family watching TV. I seem to remember *The Mary Tyler Moore Show* and *Bob Newhart*, with my head on Mom's lap. I think she started doing that at times when I was anxious, but then it continued in times of simple connection. It was a healing touch. Nothing made me feel more loved than when my mother stroked my hair. And for Rosa, long after her kittenhood was over, she showed her need for the comforting and healing touch of a mother. Perhaps we all do.

In the early twelfth century, Christian mystic Saint Bernard of Clairvaux used the word "mother" to refer to the healing presence of Jesus, as well as the biblical character of Moses, and used the term to describe the care and responsibility of abbots—who were usually called "father" by younger monks. Bernard also referred to himself, frequently, as a mother. In one letter to a wayward monk who had left the monastery, Bernard wrote, "I nourished you with milk when, while yet a child, it was all you could take. . . . But oh, how quickly you were weaned. . . . You were torn from my breast, cut from my womb. My heart cannot forget you. Half of it went with you." These words hold their intensity and even shock, now, in an era when we are so much more advanced in understanding gender.

Saint Bernard also had a great devotion to the Virgin Mary, and like many of his contemporaries, he understood her to be like a divine mother actively caring for him from the beyond. There is even a vision that Bernard is said to have undergone, in which he experienced the Virgin Mary expressing her mother's milk so that he could drink from it. Many painters have created artworks of the image, where Mary literally squirts milk into Bernard's mouth. So, the next time you're in a museum and see one of these images, now you know! Why all the motherly attention? We have motherly needs, even long after kittenhood.

Many Christian mystics also regard the human soul as feminine, so that they might understand every soul becoming a bride to the groom of God. In our own day, when understandings of gender have expanded, one of the great scholars of medieval mysticism, Bernard McGinn, said in an interview:

I like to talk about gender malleability. Gender isn't as fixed among mystics as it is in society in general. In the mystical tradition, there's a gender fluidity, and men can identify as being women and women can identify as being men. Hadewijch of Antwerp, the great thirteenth-century Flemish mystic, talks about herself as a questing knight in pursuit of God, a male categorization.

Eight hundred years ago, Saint Francis of Assisi taught that motherhood was something for all people, of any gender, to emulate—and he meant it literally. Francis did not write much, but one short document he penned was an instruction to all of his friars to spend time being "like mothers" to each other. Francis was offering guidance to his spiritual brothers, who were increasingly wishing to live in temporary, smaller communities of no more than four. This was okay with Francis, but the brothers were to take turns caring for one another. Two of them should be like children, for a while, allowing two other brothers to be like mothers on their behalf. And then, they were to exchange roles, with the "children" becoming the "mothers" and the "mothers" attending in care to the "children."

Not every mother is nurturing and loving, and many fathers have nurturing qualities. But the wisdom of Francis and the wisdom of cats remind us to pay close attention to the needs of those around us by asking, How do we show love and care for each other where we live?

To begin, watch and pay attention to the teachers you live with. I have learned that Rosa loves to be seen by me. She settles—and often naps—right in front of me, whether I'm working at my desk, making dinner, or reading a book in the living room at night. I understand this. We all want to be seen and held in view by those we love, and by those who love us. I am saddened when I come to a family mealtime and others at the table don't seem to want to look at me because they are already looking toward what they are going to do once the meal is over.

Watching and paying attention leads then to responding and using your touch. Both Rosa and Martin will often choose to be in the room where I am present. If I take my predawn coffee down to my desk in the office, which I almost always do, Martin hops up on the desk and makes his way to the window, hoping I will open it for him. Unless it is cold, I do that. And from there, he will sit for about an hour or until he hears stirring upstairs as the other humans begin to wake up. Soon, he knows that he will be fed by my daughter and moves to the next station of care. He likes his routines.

Rosa, as you know, is more of the introvert. She more often will come to the office in midday, while I am still working, and quietly make her way to my side, looking up into my eyes, and using her voice to speak her desire, which is usually for me to make room on my lap for her to jump up. Then she would like to be petted for a while, and while I'm doing that, she looks at me to be sure that I am looking back at her. It won't do for me to pet Rosa half-heartedly and keep tapping on my computer keys. She asks for my full attention. After a few minutes, I am then supposed to let her go, so that she can settle nearby, still in sight but just out of my reach. Occasionally she will find her way into the paper recycling box at my feet under the desk, making a sort of nest in there, going quickly to sleep. I can see her there, too, from where I'm sitting.

In Sanskrit there is a word, common in Hinduism, *darshan*, which simply means "seeing" but has religious connotations. Images are used in Hinduism to aid human seeing of the divine. The divine desires to be seen, and human beings naturally want to see the divine. The power of looking is intriguing to me and especially in the context of what cats teach us to understand—because there is looking and then there is being looked upon. To be looked upon is the desire of God, according to many scriptures in many religious traditions, including the Hebrew Psalms and the religious lyrics of Dravidian free verse from South India. "In your presence there is fullness and joy," sings the psalmist to God in Psalm 16:11. And as Diana Eck puts it in her short authoritative book on *darshan*: "The central act of Hindu worship, from the point of view of the lay person, is to stand in the presence of the deity and to behold the image with one's own eyes, to see and be seen by the deity." Sight and sensuality combine with belief and devotion.

We can know we are loved simply by seeing and being seen.

On days when I am not at work, sitting upstairs in the living room with that morning coffee, the cats are also almost always around. They are where I am. Or, they are where their humans are to be found. This is such a lovely quality in cat companions. I cannot say that I always share it. Sometimes, wherever the other humans are in the house, I am deliberately in another place, the places where anti-social people sometimes go. But cats remind me there are other ways to be and show love.

Some experts say that they enjoy being petted because they are being like kittens toward us in those moments, and our petting is a replacement for a mother cat's lick-ing. But this explanation seems to diminish the intimacy taking place between us—and it doesn't account for how adult cats regularly lick each other. When Martin and Rosa lick each other, they are not simply grooming one another, and they are not performing merely a cleansing function.

Humans and cats are relationship animals. Anyone who shares a house with most any example of either species will know this to be true. We look at, and touch, each other for complex and important reasons. And if you have trouble believing this about cats, consider this uncommon bit of evidence: The custom of most housecats to bury their feces, which is a gesture that experts will tell you is done out of a sensitivity to please those who live with them, because feral cats in competitive "communities" outdoors often do the precise opposite, leaving their output in a prominent place for all to experience. This also explains why some cats actually learn to use human toilets, crouching on the toilet seat to do their business; they seem to understand what we are doing when we are doing something there. The point is, like humans, cats are often signaling their willingness to be in an actively intimate and mutually respectful relationship.

Meister Eckhart, the twelfth-century Dominican mystic and preacher, used to speak of seeing and being seen by God. These are often one and the same, and they are intimately related, Eckhart used to say, to knowing and being known by God. This is because our souls are made in communion with God. There is a natural/supernatural attraction between us as humans, and between us and God. Can we see it? It doesn't always matter whether or not we can see it. We are seen nonetheless.

Cat and Human Practice

Take some time to imagine what God sees when God sees you. Is the person God sees the same one whom others know? Meister Eckhart famously said, "The eye through which I see God is the same eye through which God sees me." Meditate on this. Or, if you would rather, meditate on the well-known and similar Zen koan: "Show me your original face before you were born."

CHAPTER FOUR

Play Joyfully

Martin and Rosa often play in front of me too. They will carry a toy (a twist-tie or the plastic tag off my half-gallon of milk is all that's ever necessary) to the office in the morning and toss it in the air. Or they will chase each other around the dining room table if we as a family are all seated there. This, now, becomes the best place in the house to play this game of ours!

In some religious traditions, play is considered a godly quality, though rarely considered such in Christian communities, often known for saints and wisdom teachers valuing seriousness and intent of purpose over all else. Even Saint Francis of Assisi, my favorite of the saints, is said to have warned his friars against laughter. Yet, Francis, and many of those early Franciscans, were also at times considered holy fools, which means they were unconcerned with image and perception. It is that definition I often consider as the cats race around the family at the table, unconcerned about anything other than full-on play. In a time when public music performances were seen as frivolous or incendiary, it was Francis who would entertain people with instruments and dance far more often than he would talk about churchy things. His model for playing out were the popular French troubadours of those days, whose flamboyance and itinerancy marked them as societal outcasts, often called "fools" by both society and the church.

Saint Francis taught his followers to be fools rather than accommodate worldly things. There was the time, for instance, when Brother Juniper, one of Francis's best friends, was invited as a revered guest to a nearby town. People had heard stories of Juniper's sanctity, and they wanted to hear what he had to say. Juniper reluctantly agreed to go. But when he saw a crowd ahead on the road waiting anxiously for his arrival, he stopped to play seesaw with some children. Juniper then wouldn't leave the children no matter how confused and angry the pleading grew from the adults. He kept playing seesaw until the overserious people wanting to puff him up finally went away.

So, that not-laughing of Saint Francis did not really mean *being serious*; it meant not making fun of someone or something. It meant examining one's life, not laughing away what is important. What comes of joy and dancing—serious components of Francis's happiness—was rather a laughter of a different name.

Most people know of Saint Francis and his respect for the wildness of animals and, as such, he asked his friars not to keep pets. So there were no cats in the early friaries. Also, you may have heard that Francis was also the saint who was known to preach to birds. As the author of a lovely book called *Cloister Cats* (see "Further Reading") has said: "Followers of St. Francis and St. Clare have a particular affection for animals—though more than one person has commented, rather unfairly I think, that if St. Francis had really cared for birds, he might have done better to preach to cats!" Perhaps the answer to reconciling these things is not so difficult after all, when you consider that well-fed domestic pet cats who are allowed outdoors are responsible for the deaths of more than 2 billion songbirds in the United States alone each year.

Still, my favorite religious character for godly play is actually Krishna. In Sanskrit, the word for play is *lila*, and its origins are in the divine spontaneity that gave birth to creation itself. The idea is that *lila*, or play, began as a cosmic sport. The motive for all creation is the kind of joy that we often associate only with children who play, but there are hundreds of stories of Krishna, a form of God incarnate, told most notably in book ten of the Indian epic, *Bhagavata Purana*, as a trickster, lover, child, friend, and playmate. (And in the process even sometimes slaying demons.) It is said that, upon hearing of Krishna's antics, or that he was even just nearby, people would leave their food cooking on the stove to be near him. They were often enticed away, too, from self-centered pursuits that lead only to suffering by the beauty of Krishna's godly play. Those in this religious tradition who today practice *bhakti* yoga, the yoga of "devotion to God," listen to, read, meditate upon, or sing of the tales of Krishna.

Similar tales are not unheard of in the life of Jesus if you turn to the apocryphal gospels, such as the "Infancy Gospel of Thomas," known and read by Christians since the second century. In it, we see five-year-old Jesus playing with clay, fashioning a dozen sparrows, and then, when he is challenged by his father, Joseph, for doing this on the Sabbath (when no work was to be done), Jesus then tosses them up in the air so that they may fly away. "They went off with a squawk," the text says.

Which makes me wonder, as I look at the cats, why we haven't yet learned from them what it means to truly play, how often we are given opportunity but don't make ourselves available to each other to play. Cats desperately desire to be in each other's presence to chase, run, and play together. Why is it humans have such a hard time responding to the invitation? And why is play with our cats oftentimes easier than playing with the humans we love?

I love to love Rosa, in part, because I know that the love and the play are welcome. With the humans in my life, it isn't always so easy to show them love, to give them what I feel is love in ways they will certainly receive as love. Why is this? One reason for the difference is that with Rosa there is a transparency of feeling. She falls into my arms, for one thing, and when she does, I know how to hold her, and where to softly scratch that place behind her ears. It seems like it never fails to please her. In contrast, the humans in my life seem . . . complicated; of course they are. But even so, I know there are ways we can imitate play better than we currently do. I'm working on it. Sometimes when I'm with my cats, a blessing for play and companionship comes forth: May you feel welcome today in someone's arms. May you be petted by someone who loves you today.

Just a few moments ago, as I was writing this, my spouse called to me to come look at something quickly. There's a throw rug that Martin scampers on all day long in the living room, sitting lightly on the wooden floor. Perhaps five or six times a day I straighten it, knowing full well that he'll toss it around again soon. A few moments ago, I came at my wife's urging to look, and there was Martin in the middle of the rug, underneath it, poking only his head out so that we could see him there. I can't imagine that he didn't know this was fun, and that he did not delight in our delight looking back at him. I wonder if I ever do that for him in return. How often do I do something similar for my wife? I like to think that I could and that maybe occasionally I do.

How often do we play not just by ourselves but with and for each other? As children, we probably played in all of these ways effortlessly and naturally, but then we unlearned them when we were taught that life is serious.

I can never tell, when my cats are playing with a Ping-Pong ball trapped in a plastic cylinder, if they realize the contraption was designed so that the Ping-Pong ball will never escape that cylinder. I suspect such a realization would not matter to them. They have known from an early age how to play seriously.

Sometimes their way of playing doesn't work for me. Some cats will be petted, purring furiously, and then suddenly have enough and turn to bite their unwitting petter, or send a claw in her direction. Martin often does this. At first, I attributed it to his impetuosity or kittendom, but now I think I see that this too is part of his sense of play. I watch as he does the same thing with his sister. They will clean each other, purring, then bite and wrestle, even growl, and then return to cleaning and purring, and then maybe nap in the sun together. I don't begin to truly understand it. And since I don't have thick fur or similar claws or quite know the rules of this game that cats know best, I release Martin at the moments when he plays with me this way, wanting safety over that sort of fun and affection.

There are so many notable people in recent history who have loved to play. I like to imagine at least a few of them learned this value from cats they met or knew well.

Henry David Thoreau loved to ice skate. Albert Einstein played the violin. Dorothy Day often read novels and listened to opera on the radio. Very serious people, all for whom play taught them many lessons. Unfortunately, when many of us become adults, sometimes we stop playing. We are good at entertainment—usually involving screens and inactivity—but we have become poor players. And if we've become parents, we play with our children, but when they leave home, we again stop playing. Unless our cats keep reminding us what it means to learn to play.

Every few years I reread *Don Quixote*. As you probably know, in that classic novel, Don Quixote is an old man who lives alone and has a passion for antiquated books of chivalry, with stories of knights protecting citizens from harm and people treating each other with dignity and respect.

Books about the times when people walked the earth doing good deeds for strangers without any thought of reward. One day, Quixote decides to suit up and set out to do the same, without apparently realizing that the era for chivalric activity is gone. He doesn't seem to understand that people will think him a fool. They'll think he's playing. Don Quixote either doesn't know this or he doesn't care.

Saint Anthony, one of the first saints of the desert in antiquity, said (in effect): "A time is coming when everyone will go off-kilter, and when they see someone who isn't, they'll attack him, and say, 'You are a fool! You are not like us.'" Seventeen centuries later, it often feels like this in our world today, even as Quixotic foolishness is one of our best forms of play. Holy foolery isn't holy because the actions of the fool are holy. Holy fools don't go around feeding the hungry and clothing the naked. They may, instead, sit in the mud of a pig pen or preach to birds. Their actions are holy because they are countercultural and unexpected, sometimes even shockingly so.

The play of holy fools may seem inappropriate to too-serious people, and all of us, I suspect, are often too-serious people. Brother Juniper would sometimes deliberately humiliate himself to make a point. "Our chief illusion is our conception of ourselves, of our importance, which must not be violated, our dignity, which must not be mocked. All our resentment flows from this illusion, all our desire to do violence, to avenge insults, to assert ourselves," wrote novelist Iris Murdoch. It is this play, this "foolishness" that teaches us important lessons about priorities, humility, awe, and patience. The late twentieth-century Christian author, Henri Nouwen, once left a position teaching at Harvard to join a circus. Allow that to sink in for a moment. He tried performing as a clown and flying a trapeze. "He's a fool," people said. I expect my cats would respect that decision as very wise.

Christina the Astonishing, a Belgian twelfth-century woman, was an orphan at the age of fifteen and suffered from frequent seizures in an era when such a malady was understood as a form of mental illness. After one seizure people took her for dead and put her in a coffin. From her perch in the coffin, she then stood up. By all accounts, after that, she was unique and full of surprises. People thought they saw her, at times, hovering near the ceiling.

Christina was known to say: "My life will be astonishing, like nothing you have ever seen." And it was. Christina underwent a variety of trials and sufferings and seems to have performed some astonishing miracles. Recently scholars have wondered if she was perhaps schizophrenic, but she refused to hide the full range of herself due to any limitations or how others perceived her, and instead she inspired people, becoming a spiritual director to many who at that time were in vowed religious orders. Among the things she taught was the seriousness of the playful, surprising self.

It's a risk to be astonishing and to surprise those around us with what they may find odd—because what people find odd they often also condemn. But I think that many of us need to learn that we sometimes have to risk embarrassing our families, or ourselves, to do what is right, to play with utter seriousness. "They are a fool," people we love and respect may say about us. And that's okay. We have learned well from our mentors at play, including our cats, that we are here to play with serious intentions, to play as if it doesn't matter that the Ping-Pong ball will never leave that cylinder.

A Cat Practice

Be foolish, just a little bit. You can do it. Practice foolishness. Maybe for you that means walking backward down your sidewalk, around the block. The practice is not meant to be an exercise in feeling insecure or unsafe but, rather, a way of discovering a new vision. As you walk backward, look around you. How do things look differently than they did before? And how do people look at you differently than they did before you did this playful, turned-around thing? Does that matter to you?

Or try this—a practice that has helped me over the years. Mess up your hair and then leave it that way for at least an hour. If you are like me, and your hair usually sits in place without moving, this will cause you some discomfort. Where does this discomfort come from? How do you feel when something about you is a little unkempt, playful, wild?

CHAPTER FIVE

Eat Regularly and Well

In the previous chapters, we looked at contemplative and somewhat metaphysical matters relating to who we essentially are as human beings, as creatures and creations. We looked at some ways our cats offer us wisdom that challenge us to aspire to realize or become. We also talked a lot about love and cat wisdom in those first chapters. In this chapter, we're looking at our spiritual teachers to teach us a little more about our daily lives. Here, in chapter 5, we are all about eating a healthy bowl of kibble.

Maybe not entirely. But eating is as central to who we are as are the practices surrendering, relaxing, and loving. Martin and Rosa understand how to eat well. They seem to grasp how to feast as well as how to fast. I watch them enjoy their food, and I observe them between mealtimes forgetting entirely about food's satisfactions and distractions. We've all seen video of big cats in the wild laying around, satisfied after a good meal. My little fellow creatures do a similar post-eat chill, after we feed them well. Philosopher John Gray says rather dryly, "Since their domestication of humans, cats have not needed to rely on hunting for their food." That's true for most of our feline friends: They don't have to look far for their next meal. But they also are skilled at playing games, exploring the house—their "neighborhood"—socializing, and resting well, during the hours between feedings.

I find this instructive. As our human family struggles to even regularly sit together at coordinated mealtimes, I experience the gently insistent pull from Martin and Rosa to join them for theirs.

Every morning, why do they prefer that I watch them as they nibble breakfast from bowls in the kitchen? At first, I try to ignore Martin's not-so-gentle reminders of nibbles on my ankles and his walking around my laptop on the desk. I remain in my place. But no. Clearly, I am supposed to not simply make sure there is food in their bowls but watch as they eat at least their first few bites. As I watch, and occasionally stroke them on their backs, they purr while eating. This is *together activity*, as I know it is meant to be in our human family too.

A few months after the kittens came to us, I learned more about the work of the foster mother who cared for them in their first two months. Martin and Rosa lost their mother when they were tiny, while still nursing. So their foster human had to feed them with a bottle as frequently as a cat mother feeds its litter: every two hours. This includes doing so throughout the night. And the responsibility didn't end there. The foster mom also does for the littlest kittens one more thing that a cat mother would do, which is, after nursing, the mother cat licks the rectum of each of her kittens in order to stimulate the kitten to defecate. A kitten cannot quite do this on its own and needs a bit of help. If a foster human parent doesn't do likewise—and they do this by gently touching the rectum, usually with a warm, damp cloth—kittens can become constipated.

Observing my cats is a reminder of the role of balance in my life—spiritual, physical, and otherwise—and of the mundanity of it most of the time. We eat; we pray. We use the toilet; we express love to one another. Our lives are made of these daily things.

Sometimes we grow bored, wanting to punctuate the tenacious regularity of spiritual practice and discipline, and our boredom steers us off course with mild rebellions. Sometimes that's okay, but I find I am most happy when I allow myself to settle into the regularity itself—when I am willing to let go of expectations (mine, as well as those of others) that a life well-lived is a life of frequent excitement. It's simply not true. And our cats, who benefit in well-being from a good routine, seem to understand that too.

There is joy and happiness in walking a steady path. By doing so, we replace the ups and the downs, religious highs and lows, with regular skills and practices. Martin and Rosa's eating, playing, and napping remind me of these lessons. Your cat companions share these lessons as well, if you pay attention.

Teresa of Avila, one of my favorite Catholic mystics, was known to plead, "Lord, save me from gloomy saints!"

She also once said in response to a convent visitor who was surprised that the sisters were about to eat a seemingly extravagant meal, "There's a time for partridge and a time for penance." Good meals are good for you, in more ways than one. Then, forgetting about food is good for you, as well. It can be difficult, particularly at times when we're unable to leave the house or are stuck at our desk for hours on end, to forget about the satisfactions of food and other pleasurable things. We keep nibbling the kibble.

Cats become antsy when they get hungry, as humans are prone to do. As I do. I sometimes refer to these overly antsy hungry cat moments as "eating the lamps." In fact Martin and Rosa have done exactly that—nibbled on our lampshades when I've forgotten to feed them. They seem to use this as a way of communicating, *Hey, human!* They are anxious to use their teeth for eating, and they are saying to me that they have stretched a bit beyond their reasonable fasting limit. I try to listen and pay attention. It is my duty to feed them. It is my job, our job, to feed each other. Just as it's also our responsibility to eat what is responsibly ours.

In Sunni Islam the fourth pillar echoes similar teachings in Judaism and Christianity about the necessity of fasting. This pillar is also central to Muslim life in ways that it is perhaps less so to the other two Abrahamic faiths.

Fasting isn't a popular part of any religious tradition today because people assume it is a negative practice: (1) don't eat and (2) religious obligation forbids it. But we're missing something essential.

One aspect of fasting in Sunni Islam—as well as in my own lay, monastic-style Catholicism—is finding the balance and all-round blessings of both enjoyable eating and regular hunger. There are many good reasons for keeping this balance. For those of us with plenty, regular hunger reminds us of others who don't have; it also maintains our equilibrium closer to the mean of humanity, curbing the ways that our rich-in-resources lifestyles might otherwise tend toward excess. The French philosopher and writer Simone Weil, who came from privilege, spent long periods of time as an adult fasting in solidarity with those who had little or nothing to eat. Likewise, your sheikh, rabbi, or priest will perhaps remind you that we fast at regular times throughout the year in order to remember what it feels like to "hunger" for God. That resonates with me, as I feel that way during fasting times.

There is a beautiful Hasidic tale of the Baal Shem Tov, the founder of Hasidism, taking food with him on a spiritual retreat, and realizing only after the fact, days later, that he hadn't touched it. Martin Buber tells it like this:

When the Baal Shem Tov was young, he used to take six loaves of bread and a pitcher of water at the close of the sabbath, when he went into seclusion for the entire week. On a Friday, when he was ready to go home, and about to lift his sack from the ground, he noticed that it was heavy, opened it, and found all the loaves still in it. He was very much surprised.

This possibility is also what the Sufi commentator communicates when he says, slightly adapted here, "God feeds the elect of God's servants who spend the night with God, not with themselves nor creation, just as the Prophet said, 'I spend the night with my Lord feeding me and giving me to drink.'"

But fasting doesn't have to be religious. For Simone Weil, fasting was not a part of a religious ritual. For her, with her radical commitment to identifying with the poor, it was the most basic way of knowing that we are all the same. You cannot have a meaningful feast without also allowing yourself at times to be genuinely and completely hungry. We're all the same in our deepest needs and joys. We all "eat the lamps," indicating to ourselves and others that we understand both the filling and the emptying.

Qur'an 2:183 says, "Fasting is prescribed for you as it was prescribed for those before you, that haply you may be reverent" (*The Study Quran*). One of the older translations broadens it, with more of a spiritual promise that every seeker-person can relate to: "O you who believe, fasting is prescribed for you as it was prescribed for those before you, that you may develop God-consciousness."

Some people are drawn to reverencing God, worship, and gratitude. What if those acts, and that posture (for lack of a better word), also created something in us: God-consciousness? Maybe Martin and Rosa aren't aware of these purposes or benefits of fasting. But they fast all the same. They understand the rhythm of eating, the feeling of want. We and they appreciate our meals and then we put the food away for a time to focus on other things.

To Practice

If you don't already, and health permitting, you may wish to try this week a twelve- to thirteen-hour fast each day from the end of your last meal until breakfast the following morning. Treat this as a fast, in all that means for you. The word "fast" comes from an Old English word meaning "firm" and "steadfast." Be that, for at least twelve hours, relating to food.

Then, you may wish to watch (or watch again) the 1987 Danish film, "Babette's Feast." It is beautiful in its understanding of the daily, the extraordinary. Before you watch you might want to read the review on the Spirituality and Practice website: https://www.spiritualityandpractice.com/films/reviews/view/5021/babettes-feast. Because just as it is good to fast, it is good for us to also know how to *feast*—which is a word derived from Old French and Latin meaning "joyous."

CHAPTER SIX

Sit in the Sun

On any given afternoon, Martin and Rosa will find the sunniest place in the house and sprawl in it. After an hour or longer in such a place, they look so completely at ease, at home, in their bodies and in their surroundings. I envy them in this. Not that I want to relocate to Florida or a beach somewhere but that I would simply like to feel that comfortable.

My responsibilities keep me from doing what they do, on most days, or at least that is my usual excuse: that I don't have time to luxuriate. But I also think there is more to it than simply being comfortable from a lack of responsibility. Watching the cats in their warm places reminds me of times when I, too, have experienced wondrous warmth and prayed with heat.

I'm not a Sun-God worshipper. Ancient Africa and Greece, and Aztec mythology, offer rich images of sun deities. But I *am* a worshipper, a pray-er, in the sun. The ancients knew something that we humans often forget, something my cats seem to simply intuit: A place in the sun is like a place with God. Each of us needs the warmth and to experience it directly. Sunshine's heat can't be gotten from the descriptions of others, and looking to others to tell us about the sun's warmth always stands in the way of our understanding.

Ecclesiastes (the book in the Bible from which the Byrds took their lyrics for "Turn! Turn! Turn!" in 1965) offers typically wise advice: "If two lie down together, they will keep warm. But how can one keep warm alone?" We are warmer and stronger together rather than by ourselves. But a cat in the sun reminds me of something more personal and more accurate that reflects both, somehow: If you lie down alone, you are in fact not alone—you are lying down with God. The warmth of sunshine reminds me of this.

St. Hildegard of Bingen, the medieval German abbess and mystic, believed in the Holy One who is constantly "greening" the world and who relates to her/his creations with vibrancy and warmth. How does that greening take place but with abundant sunshine? In Matthew Fox's translation, from his book *Original Blessings*, Hildegard hears God saying: "With my mouth, I kiss my own chosen creation. I uniquely, lovingly embrace every creation I have made out of the earth's clay. With a fiery spirit I transform it into a body to serve all the world." We may be able to feel this kiss most of all when we are like a cat on a sun-warmed tiled floor.

Another of the great Christian female mystics, Saint Teresa of Avila, said: "The things of the soul must always be considered as plentiful, spacious, large. . . . The soul is capable of much more than we imagine, and the sun that is in this royal chamber shines in all parts." In her analogy, each soul is able to spend time in the royal chamber of the Holy One, and the Royal One heats and lights up that soul chamber like the sun.

There are other means of warmth connected to the spiritual life. I think of sweat lodges in Indigenous spiritual traditions for healing and connecting with the Creator. Sweat lodges originated with Indigenous and First Nation peoples of the Great Plains, including tribal communities such as Lakota, Blackfoot, and Crow. I am most familiar with the Lakota tradition—its past leaders include some of the most important figures in the history of what is now the North American continent: Sitting Bull, Red Cloud, Crazy Horse, and Nicholas Black Elk, about whom I recently wrote a biography.

In those traditions, one enters a Lakota sweat lodge with the intention of spiritual cleansing and purification. The sweat isn't accidental, but it is also not the sole purpose of the exercise. The best comparison I can make, in other religious traditions, is to a pilgrimage: Both are physical, involving exercise and even exhaustion (when done well), prompting a kind of intentionally helpless and unavoidable humility. Both practices cost you something that is both physical and spiritual. Also, both sweat lodge and pilgrimage are experiences of being part of something bigger than yourself. I think of Malcolm X's accounts of the Hajj, the Muslim pilgrimage to Mecca, and how he was forever changed afterward, beyond the racial exclusivism he had been taught by his teachers. He wrote in a letter at that time: "I have never before witnessed such sincere hospitality and the practice of true brotherhood as I have seen it here in Arabia. In fact, all I have seen and experienced on this pilgrimage has forced me to 're-arrange' much of my thought-patterns previously held, and to toss aside some of my previous conclusions." This is the heat of spiritual cleansing.

A sweat lodge is also a dark place: Animal hides are used to cover bunches of willow (bendable) trees, made to form a lodge shape. From the outside, it looks like a big turtle. Hot rocks, or coals, inside create the heat. People go in and sit to rest, rejuvenate, heal.

There is a fear of darkness, and a sense of foreboding relating to darkness, that I think often keep some of us from enjoying light as simple sunshine. The poet William Blake, for instance, praises the rising sun over and over again. He writes, at several points, of seeing a heavenly host in the sunshine, crying, "Holy, holy, holy!" like the angels in the book of Isaiah. Blake's praise and characterizations of sunshine are so over the top, at times, that I worry how he must have felt on cloudy days.

And as much as I watch them in their sun sitting, I don't know what Martin and Rosa are thinking as they lay there in the window, or on the floor, in that patch of afternoon sun. For all I know, they too are rejuvenating and healing. But I think they have a much quieter understanding of the sun and its role for their lives. I've watched them sometimes for an hour or more, lying there in the warm rays. It is as if the sun works through them the way that a good massage therapist works through the sinews and muscles of a human body. Except that all Martin and Rosa seem to need is what's already within them, and sunshine.

For every creature under heaven, the sun is our warmth and to consciously be in it is one of the most basic gifts we are given. It is a place to pray. We all need warm places to remind us to pray and to remind us that we are with God.

Sometimes, too, a warm place is a companion in a time of need. I think of the day recently when I had an intense earache, my whole head pounding and ringing. I didn't want to talk to anyone or answer questions. The presence I sought when I was feeling awful was Rosa's. She sat still on the bed while I laid my sore head next to her warm body. She must have remained there with me for an hour. Could she have known I was in pain and she was of such great help to me? I wonder.

By the time I was feeling better, ready to move from that place, I realized that we had been lying together in the sun.

A Cat Practice

It is not always easy to find a place in the sun, especially in winter, but hopefully wherever you are and whenever you read this, you may be able to do so. Find a sunny place and sit or stand there for at least two or three minutes. Give this practice fifteen minutes if you can. Feel the warmth of the sunshine on your skin. Allow yourself to luxuriate in the warmth, if you can. Lie down. Or sit half-lotus. Bow your head. Raise your palms. Do whatever it is that you do to both rest in your body and raise your attention to the universe around you.

Then, consider praying these words, slightly adapted from the "Sun Prayer" of Father Charles Flood, SCJ (d. 1995), a Congregation of the Sacred Heart priest who lived and worked among the Lakota people:

> Great Spirit, God and Father, be the center of my life today. You fill all the emptiness of space. May the sun today be a healthy healing warmth for me that I, in turn, may become healer of other's hurts.

CHAPTER SEVEN

Voice Your Opinion

Many times, I've heard people praise the obedience of dogs against the independent spirit of cats to make a point about what God asks of human beings. I've heard them argue not just that dogs are good and cats are bad, but that dogs are righteous and cats are evil. I'm not kidding. One recent blog posting went like this: "Dogs will do whatever it takes to please their masters. Cats will do whatever it takes to please themselves. Though we may smile about the difference between these two, it's really no laughing matter."

This is a very shallow understanding of faith and spirituality, even for Christians. Abraham argued with God, leading to a change of God's mind (Genesis 18). Moses did likewise (Exodus 32). Even Jesus Christ, from the cross, argues with God (Matthew 27:46). So don't tell me faith means being quietly obedient like a trained dog. I don't believe this is even a worthy goal.

The independence of cats is precisely what many of us love about them and can relate to. On the whole, cats are not as trainable as dogs. They don't jump with obedience or respond easily to simple rewards and punishments. In other words, they are more like most of us.

One afternoon a few years ago, my wife was walking our dog, Max, in our neighborhood. Max, of blessed memory, was a large mutt, a mix with some Rottweiler, black with a large jaw, and sweet as could be—to women and children. Max was a rescue dog, and he must have been abused by a large man when he was a pup, because he was always and only nervous around large men. He would become tense and unhinged when we were walking down the sidewalk and a large man approached. Those were embarrassing moments for us. Hopefully, the men we passed on the sidewalk simply thought that we had a nervous or upset dog.

So many great dogs and cats begin as rescues, and I hope that if you turn from this book of mine to find a cat of your own to love, that you too will turn first to a shelter to rescue your own. Unless you are able to do the rescuing yourself, firsthand. One exceptional rescue story comes in the first chapter of Cleveland Amory's classic book, *The Cat Who Came for Christmas.* Probably the best-selling book ever about a cat or cats, it begins its first chapter, appropriately titled, "The Rescue," with an account of Cleveland setting sight on his beloved—"He was thin and he was dirty and he was hurt"—on the streets of New York one Christmas Eve. Among rescue stories is also one I wrote in a book for children called *The Pope's Cat,* where my fictional pope stumbles upon a stray while out for a walk on the Via della Conciliazione in Rome one morning. He picks her up and tucks her in his cassock and adopts her, carrying her back inside the Vatican.

But that's not the story of this particular afternoon and Max, who bolted his leash at the sight of a large man jogging down the median. My wife was surprised by the sudden tug of the leash, losing hold of her end. Unfortunately, the jogger was someone who is afraid of dogs, and Max's appearance certainly didn't help in this regard. So the jogger ran faster than before, chased by Max, while yelling. The great irony of dog behavior with humans is that they tend to hurt those who are most sensitive to the possibility of being hurt. A dog gets frightened by the feeling of fear in others. So Max ran hard and soon, despite my wife's running after him and pleading as best she could in a bid to get him back under control, Max nipped the jogger in the butt. It was dramatic, but the good news is the event didn't result in an injury beyond torn sweatpants and a bruised ego. The fear in the jogger was so profound that after being nipped, he immediately insisted that our dog "be put down," even writing a letter to city authorities about this. My wife had to plead for Max's life and thankfully succeeded.

Where did this notion come from, that a dog who acts like an animal and hurts a human being must immediately and without discussion be killed? In our case what happened was a mandatory interview of Max by a local animal control official, who found Max in fine dog order. Blessed Max lived with us for many more years, but he still occasionally became nervous around large men, especially those jogging. We held his leash much tighter.

We rarely say the same about a cat. A cat feeling cornered is roughly the equivalent of a dog feeling teased into chasing a skateboarder or jogger. If that frightened cat scratches someone, even if it results in human blood, we don't conclude that it must be "put down." We reason that the cat was scared, and we should do better not to put the cat into that situation. I have known cats for whom earlier traumatic experiences mean that their humans care for them giving wide latitude, of necessity and with sensitivity.

Perhaps because a dog is supposed to be trained and then do what it is told, it is deemed dangerous when and if it does otherwise. I'm not sure.

The late twentieth-century Russian poet Wisława Szymborska once said: "Whatever inspiration is, it's born from a continuous 'I don't know.'" I hope my ongoing questions about dogs and cats offer up inspiration.

I prefer to give our animal companions the room they need and sometimes demand. When Martin and Rosa walk away from me with defiance, I don't think less of them. In fact, there is a recent study of cat attachment behavior with human companions that demonstrates this principle in ways that illumine how cats who are secure in their human connections behave. Most experts will say that pet cats look upon their human companions as larger cats, in contrast to how pet dogs look to their humans, which is as an other-species "alpha" creature. After a period of several minutes away from their human caretaker, once reunited, cats with the least amount of stress and separation distress were not the ones who went directly to their human's lap, and they were not the ones who walked around the room in which their human sat, waiting, in avoidance of them. Instead, the best-adjusted cats were those that looked at their human, tail swaying in the air, and walked just within about an arm's-length reach.

Animal behavior, and differences between species aside, let's state it plainly: Doglike obedience in humans is not Christian. It's also not Jewish.

As the spouse of a rabbi, I've come to know the work of a network of rabbis and cantors called T'ruah. As they explain: "The name T'ruah—one of the sounds of the sho-far (ram's horn)—calls us to take action to create a more just world and indicates our belief in the possibility of liberation." And that's their work—to mobilize Jews and their allies for justice and to defend human rights: Fighting antisemitism, aiding asylum seekers and refugees, creating a better future for Israelis and Palestinians, ending solitary confinement, ending mass incarceration, exposing human trafficking and enslavement, and creating sanctuary spaces in synagogues around the world.

Martin and Rosa don't fight for human rights, but they demonstrate with their lives how not to have their lives ordered around my expectations. They are great companions in my home, but they also show how being good and doing good is not always the same as being well-behaved.

What's the saying?—*Well-behaved women rarely make history.* Consider the Nuns on the Bus, which is the name of one of the many campaigns of "Network Advocates for Justice, Inspired by Catholic Sisters." They are Roman Catholic women, members of religious orders, who organize Catholics and other allies to educate and lobby in areas such as food security, equal access to health care, immigration reform, and restorative justice. When obedience means acquiescence, they are clear that it is not a positive value. Disobedience can be godly. But to those human creatures who are taught to sit up and beg and acquiesce and be obedient and say yes, yes, yes, it will never occur to them to disobey.

Daniel Berrigan, SJ, the Jesuit priest and poet who protested against the draft during the Vietnam War and went to jail for justice on numerous occasions, said in *The Geography of Faith*, "The world is full of suffering and exploitation, and that fact keeps one in touch with the realities that make one's behavior a moral challenge."

Each day when Martin and Rosa remind me they won't exactly do what I want, I remember the spiritual value of knowing your lines but then disobeying when the situation calls for something beyond yesses and obedience.

Human Practice

Sister Simone Campbell, the most recognizable of the Nuns on the Bus, recommends "holy curiosity" as a way to make a difference in your neighborhood around issues of justice. She talks of how she does this:

> There are not many places where I stand in line, but one place where I do is the grocery store. . . . I like to begin a conversation by asking the person in front of or behind me a question

about current events in order to learn that person's perspective. I will ask if she or he has an opinion about rising wages, expanding health care, or voter suppression. I will ask about anything that is on my mind and in my heart and then listen to the response. . . . Practicing holy curiosity is one small step toward reweaving the fabric of our society.

This holy curiosity is so simple. We can all do this. And it seems like a good small step in the right direction.

CHAPTER EIGHT

Keep to a Schedule

Discipline and self-discipline are unpopular, almost countercultural ideas. Many of us grew up in homes where discipline was imposed in such a way that we grew to adulthood thinking we'd earned the right to be free of it, like a prisoner who is finally free of constraints. But self-discipline—and discipline itself—are not constraining when they are a healthy part of a life of spiritual practice. In fact, discipline remains essential for anyone to keep on a spiritual path.

No one falls into a life of meaning accidentally or haphazardly, and no one who pursues the opposite values of meaning in life is on a spiritual path. Attention, deliberation, action, and purpose are markers along the road, and on that road, the guardrails are disciplines we use to keep us there.

A typical day in my house sees Martin and Rosa sitting up with me for vigils in the early morning hours before the sun awakens. Some Psalms, the occasional contemplative groan, and frequent prayer darts thrown into the air fill my heart and come quietly out of my mouth. Beside me, usually, my cats sit, even as I practice aligned with the call of texts like this one from the book of Lamentations: "Arise, cry out in the night, at the beginning of the watches! Pour out your heart like water before the presence of the Lord!" This is what we do, only without the sound that the exclamation point might indicate.

All three of us are awake, earlier than our physicians would say we should be, and we are a little bit hungry, but we don't sleep and we don't eat. First, we sit together in the darkness. And I pray words such as these from Psalm 51: "You desire truth in the inward being; therefore teach me wisdom in my secret heart."

We keep saying lines from the Psalms, as we join with other contemplatives and monastics around the world who are also sitting up and praying at night. We? Well, at least I imagine that the cats are doing this with me. They seem patient enough.

(And on the occasional mornings when I am not out of bed on time, before the dawn, I open the bedroom door and there are Martin and Rosa, looking expectantly at me, like, *What do you think you're doing, getting up so late? It's time for psalms.*)

We practice this little bit of self-discipline, beginning with prayers and not immediately jumping to the food bowl, to remind our minds and bodies that there is more to life than what nourishes our cells. Our spirits animate us, and they are coming alive in the early-morning hours in ways that are just as important. I remember a teaching from Saint Teresa of Avila, a Spanish Carmelite mystic of the sixteenth century who counseled many wannabe contemplatives and experienced her own set of failures in the spiritual life: "There are some souls and minds so scattered they are like wild horses no one can stop. Now they're running here, now there, always restless."

So, we stay settled and we keep mostly quiet. We need this to begin our day. As Saint Edith Stein once taught, "Becoming empty and still are closely connected. The soul is replenished by nature in so many ways that one thing always replaces another, and the soul is in constant agitation, often in tumult and uproar."

Once the sun does come up, Martin and Rosa continue to assist me in other ways in the practice of discipline. They insist I remain on task, at least in terms of keeping to their feeding schedule and giving them loving attention at the usual times. So, just as we have our contemplative routine in the morning dark, we maintain a routine in when and how we eat each morning, breaking the night's fast together.

If you live with animals, you know how important this kind of companionship can be for maintaining good routines and habits in your own life. I would not be as good at prayer, contemplation, and the practice of lectio divina, or spiritual reading, without the persistent reminders that come from my felines.

When our beloved dog, Max, died two years ago, we realized something similar had been knitted into part of our routine and spiritual well-being. With Max gone, my wife and I stopped taking thoughtful and deliberate walks every morning and afternoon. She usually wakes up after me, and part of her mourning Max's loss was to mourn the loss of the reason she got out of bed in the morning. An important piece of her discipline was suddenly gone with Max.

But it's more than just praying and eating and walking; what I find so helpful about Martin and Rosa's presence in my life is how they encourage me to stay on course and show me how discipline in small ways can influence my whole day for the good.

One of my favorite contemporary spiritual teachers, Christine Valters Paintner, says: "The practice of a spiritual discipline is about more than the minutes we spend doing it, but how it overflows into the whole of life." Morning prayer, good eating, and thoughtful walking spread into every corner of my living, making me feel good in body and soul, increasing my happiness and well-being. Martin and Rosa demonstrate the value and the priority of regularity in my practice. Creatures of habit and routine, they teach me how to be so as well.

Once, for example, by the time they reached their first birthday, I realized that Martin was unduly stressed when hungry. We were not leaving food out at all times but keeping them to specific mealtimes. But Martin began to show the signs of a cat experiencing stress at this change. He would become aggressive, beyond playful, and he would even occasionally mark his displeasure around the house by spraying. Since he was neutered, this spraying wasn't so bad, and it had relatively little odor, but it was an indication that he was stressed out.

So I decided to begin leaving food out at all times. Just a little bit extra. *No worries!* I was saying to him with my actions. Except that Martin is also really good at developing habits and patterns—so for months after this small change, he would still wake me up at four o'clock in the morning to feed him. (More on this in the next chapter.) At first, I would walk with him downstairs to his bowl and somewhat sarcastically exclaim, "See, Martin?! Look, there's food there!" But that wasn't enough. For months, I had to place a few more pieces into the nuggets already in the bowl to make that you're-being-fed sound that Martin seems to find so comforting. Then he'd begin to nibble away on it, and I would be able to go back to bed.

Or, I wouldn't. Staying up and staying awake are such good practices for me. I was monastically inclined before the cats arrived, and during the pandemic they were like monks beside me in the abbey choir, encouraging me to do what I ought to do and what I truly want to do, instead of all those other ways I might steer off course, wasting my time.

The cycle begins again the next morning, and every morning before sunup, and I find that it feeds everything else in my life.

A friend of mine, Trappist monk Brother Paul Quenon, has a poem titled "Watchman" in which he captures just right the spirit of disciplined attention to something so indeterminate as praying in the darkness in the middle of the night to a God we cannot hope to see. The poem includes these lines, as Brother Paul imagines an interlocutor questioning him on why he does something so seemingly small and meaningless: "What do you watch? / Nothing." This is followed by, "Then why watch? / Haven't found nothing yet." Those lines make me smile, and they explain a lot with so few words.

The "practice" in "spiritual practice" is about doing it daily, or at least with disciplined regularity. Like good friends and partners, Martin and Rosa don't allow me to be undisciplined. They insist that I cultivate attention on their behalf but also for my own good, and for that I'm thankful.

The practice of spirituality is also rarely ever a sprint. It is more of a long-distance walk.

This came home to me recently while I was shoveling snow on a bitterly cold day at our house in Milwaukee. I like snow, and I actually like shoveling, to a point. But this was the first shoveling of what I knew would be two or three visits to the sidewalk that day, because we were in the midst of a Great Lakes blizzard.

Anyone who has spent time shoveling snow knows how after a few weeks of working it, when there's been no thaw between snowfalls, the shoveled snow begins to pile up. Sometimes you even begin to run out of places to put it. Don't toss it far enough and it will fall back down onto the sidewalk, doubling your work.

So, on this morning, for those reasons (knowing that more was coming that day and the piles were already going high), I was tossing the snow with a bit more umph, knowing that doing so was good for me in the long run. As I did so, it hit me: this is like prayer. The work I do now is to clear the sidewalk, but it is also to clear the sidewalk by making room for what will come soon to fill the sidewalk again. The work never ends, but that puts it too negatively. I think of it as my good work now that helps make possible my good work later.

Practice for Cats and Humans

Whether at night, after sundown, or in the early morning before sunrise, take fifteen or twenty minutes this week and sit in the dark and see what you can and cannot see. Sit quietly. Hopefully, you can find fifteen or twenty uninterrupted minutes wherever you find yourself. As you sit there in the dark, look at objects in the house and at things outside, through the windows. Observe them closely, in detail, one by one. Take note of what you see. Next, consider how things appear differently to you in the dark. What insights can you take into the day with you?

CHAPTER NINE

Wake Up

About a year into our time with our kittens, there was a period of weeks when Martin would consistently wake me up between three and four o'clock in the morning. At first, this was adorable. He would wander in and out of our bedroom during the night. Our kittens were playful but mostly quiet. Sometimes I would be gently and somnambulantly aware of this activity, and sometimes not. That was fine.

Then, it became something else. When he reached about a year old, in the smack dead of our sleep, Martin would perform a big jump onto the bed. *Thump.* He wasn't a kitten anymore. By this point, he was a little athlete and weighed eight pounds. And he also wasn't trying to be quiet. The thump alone was usually enough to surprise me awake, and I think he cleverly figured that out. He knew I sleep fairly light. Always have, since becoming a father some thirty years ago. But at his full-grown weight and attitude, Martin wasn't jumping onto the bed in the middle of the night simply to lie down and sleep beside us. Even that would have been fine.

In the dark I would feel him walking directly over me—usually starting on my legs, making his way up my hip or backside. Once there, he would pause for a moment. *Is the human stirring yet?* Then, shortly, it was onto my neck. It was as if Martin was simply going for a stroll, and if I lay in the bed pretending that I wasn't noticing, and hoping that maybe he'd go away soon, Martin would stop at my neck. He would sit. And purr.

The first few weeks he did this, I honestly didn't mind so much. It was mostly cute, and the sun was soon to rise anyway. I enjoy Martin's company. Also, perhaps I mentioned that I've been a parent of children for three decades? That means I haven't slept well for a very long time, and that's mostly okay. I have become accustomed to waking often and early. There are good things waking me up, and I have learned over the years to value, rather than dread and avoid, the early-morning hours.

Thich Nhat Hanh teaches a lesson familiar in most every religious tradition in one form or another, about finding the spiritual lesson and truth close to home, right where you are. In Thay's version, this lesson comes in the form of a warning:

> [T]he treasure we are looking for remains hidden to us. Stop being like the man in the Lotus Sutra who looked all over the world for the gem that was already in his pocket. Come back and receive your true inheritance. Don't look outside yourself for happiness. Let go of the idea that you don't have it. It is available within you.

My early-morning waking became this, for me, many years ago: An opportunity for blessings rather than a source of anxiety. Domestic life is full of these opportunities to make what seem at first to be inconveniences, into trainings—and often, gifts.

The cats are among my trainers. In fact, the smallest things continue to wake me. My four human children have always known that Dad is the parent to approach in the middle of the night if you have a problem. Mom is usually totally lights out, but Dad is quick to rise. So, when Martin woke me before four o'clock, I was most likely about to wake up anyway. It was okay. But when night by night four o'clock became closer to three o'clock, and then became even earlier than that, we had a problem that needed to be fixed. I don't need to keep watch with the night quite that early.

At first it seemed to be about food. Martin was anxious when his bowl was empty, and he did not want to wait until morning light to see it filled. So, I began brimming it before bed every evening. Surely, then, he wouldn't have reason to wake me like this. But he still apparently did. After a while I think he was simply bored and knew from experience that I am the one in the house who will be stirred enough not to sleep any longer. The funny thing was that, most often, by the time I was clearly awake, sitting up and beginning to think about what needed to be done and the priorities of the morning, Martin had put himself back to sleep, often back in the warm part of our bed, where he had found me.

The quality of our being awake matters. Waking is not only about opening our eyes, sitting up, using the toilet, eating, or drinking, which are all things we eventually do when we get up. Waking up is saying, *Here I am.* There is perhaps no one to hear us say it, except for ourselves, and still there is meaning in our willing readiness.

Waking up is also for more than ourselves. Waking is for turning our attention outside ourselves. The religious traditions agree on this point. Christians will remember the vision of Jesus given in the Gospel of Matthew, chapter 25, where human beings are separated like sheep from goats at the end of life, according to the deeds they have done to help other people. The Qur'an has something similar:

> There is none in the heavens and on the earth, but that it comes unto the Compassionate as a servant. He has taken account of them, and numbered them exactly. And each of them shall come unto Him on the Day of Resurrection, alone. Surely those who believe and perform righteous deeds, for them shall the Compassionate ordain love.

For many of us, the days of belief in an afterlife, especially one containing divine rewards and punishments, is past. Maybe, as I see it, instead the afterlife is a beautiful, karmic interpretation of the old idea of afterlife consequences; the suggestion is that there is more than the afterlife to concern our interest in awakening. "Surely those who believe and perform righteous deeds, for them shall the Compassionate ordain love."

And this returns us, again, to where we started—it's all about waking up. Not waking up in the middle of the night. Not waking up from sleep. But waking up in ways that resemble in our hearts and souls what our bodies are doing when we rise from the night's rest. The Zen Buddhist idea of waking up is most of all about breaking the spell of falsity that usually runs our lives like a play that we star in and imagine others are watching, but it is really only fooling us into playing a character instead of being who we are. Zen teacher Bonnie Myotai Treace explains this beautifully:

> Most people will find that their attachment with ego is like a spell that gets broken each time they engage in genuine practice. An alternative begins to wake up in the heart-mind—a glimpse of something truer, more honest. Breaking from the ego-trance, even momentarily, wakes up a bone-deep calmness: The tension of pretending can be let go, again and again.

So, wake up with me. And Martin.

Human Practice

Are you familiar with the Jewish practice of blessings?

A blessing is not a prayer, particularly if by prayer you mean asking God for something. A blessing (in Hebrew, a *bracha*) is simply a recognizing of goodness, beauty, abundance, truth, and gift. And "recognizing" is important—because it cannot be done unless we are awake. We recognize best when we use more than our mind and lips but other senses as well. So, the idea of blessings is to wake up every part of us.

Take a few minutes to sit up. Open your eyes. Or if you're able, stand. In Judaism, traditional blessings begin with the words, *Baruch ata Adonai* . . . , or "Blessed are you, God . . . ," followed by naming one aspect of the goodness, beauty, abundance, truth, and gift that we recognize in our lives. Feel free to change the name you give to God; just say some blessings today.

CHAPTER TEN

Sit Your Ground

When I see Rosa and Martin sitting so quietly, without movement or care, near me, I want to feel like I imagine they feel. I would like to settle down, with my passions dispersed and diffused all around me like a cat on a couch. Or curled up on the floor. Or on a messy pile on my desk. Or most anywhere they can find. If I could do this from time to time, I believe I would become a more compassionate person.

One of the ways I am learning that relaxed quiet, that compassion, is from Roshi Joan Halifax, one of the hidden gems of Buddhist teaching in the United States for many decades. If you don't know her or have not experienced her wisdom, I encourage you to do that soon. She has shared a nine-minute "Meditation on Compassion" that offers a set of letting-go's that are profound:

First, "Let go of external distractions," Roshi Joan tells us, as her meditation begins. Over and over, she emphasizes, let go of those things that distract you on each inhaling breath, and on each exhale, begin to relax.

"Allow yourself to be grounded and present," she says, encouraging the work of the breath. And then, when you're ready, "Recall your intention—really, why you are here." Then, if you're ready, "Notice what feelings are present."

I don't know what Rosa and Martin are feeling. I can't of course know that for sure. But I know how I feel when they look at me in these moments of calm presence. There is such a feeling of acceptance and affection between us. I wish there were more human beings who looked at me in that way from time to time. I wish I knew how to look at other people in that way too.

At the same time, who knows for sure? "So often they are standing completely still. Yet when I look up again a few minutes later, they are in another place, again standing completely still. . . . Their attention is complete, as they look across the road: They are still, and face us. Just because they are so still, their attitude seems philosophical," writes essayist Lydia Davis in her beautiful little chapbook about the creatures she looks to for creaturely wisdom, cows. But I think it is more than that; they are standing still, and in their stillness, they are more than philosophical. They have the very qualities of one who meditates. Some might say, a cow doesn't or cannot have qualities in them that meditation requires of one. To that I simply say, How do you know? But in Roshi Joan's meditation, we can hold the pause, together:

"Notice what feelings are present," Roshi Joan says. I know today that I need to open my heart to someone. I won't name them, but believe me when I say that my heart has been closed to someone in recent weeks. I respond with anger when their name comes up because they have hurt me in the past. They probably hurt me because they, too, are hurting. I am going to try and look at them in a new way, with compassionate eyes and a compassionate heart.

To "sit your ground" is, I think, to do the work necessary to see the truth. Our sight is distorted if we are constantly moving and rushing and keeping to a quick schedule of appointment and achievement. We have to take regular time, like Rosa and Martin do, to sit. Just sit, and as every good teacher of meditation will instruct, allow yourself to be grounded and present.

Sitting your ground is also about doing the work yourself. There are times to lean on others, and then there are times when it is best to find our own roots and grounding. Philosopher John Gray suggests that one of the lessons cats teach us is to avoid unhealthy and dysfunctional connections with other people. Just as a cat does not appear to need you in order to find inner peace and satisfaction, so you do not need others to find the same inside of you. John Gray writes, "Beware [of] anyone who offers to make you happy," writing that,

> Those who offer to make you happy do so in order that they themselves may be less unhappy. Your suffering is necessary to them, since without it they would have less reason for living. Mistrust people who say they live for others.

But in giving and receiving love, there is something else, beyond the offer of happiness based on certain conditions. In her book *Help Thanks Wow*, Anne Lamott says this amazing thing: "Love pulls people back to their feet. New blades of grass grow from charred soil. The sun rises." I think you'll find that this leads to happiness, as well. As you sit, you will realize what is essential to your life: what you have that cannot be held in your hands, and it will make you smile.

Then, gratitude will rise in you too. Even if you're suffering—and so many are—if you sit your ground, knowing who you essentially are as beloved of the divine and belonging to all, feelings of thanks will ascend. As Brother David Steindl-Rast teaches, "If we are not grateful, then no matter how much we have, we will not be happy, because we will always want to have something else or something more."

All those times when Martin and Rosa relax in a spirit of profound quiet, I am reminded that life is giving and affirming. We are reminded, by gratitude, that we're always able to learn something about contentment and sitting our ground, too.

To Practice

Roshi Joan Halifax's "Meditation on Compassion"can be found on YouTube: https://www.youtube.com/watch?v= JHaaIw5y8jU. I shared a few moments from the meditation but encourage you to give yourself those nine minutes in compassion today. After you have practiced the meditation, you might ask yourself: What feelings are present as you sit and listen to her teaching? Then, find a friend with whom you can discuss what it means for you to sit your ground.

CHAPTER ELEVEN

Refuse to Be Tamed

Earlier we looked at one of the negative things people sometimes say about cats, as a way of contrasting cats with dogs. There's quite a list of other things that people use to create comparisons. Among them are these.

It is said that dogs will never leave your side, they are faithful, and they will always come when you call, whereas your cat will come and go as she pleases.

It is said that dogs are more "useful" than cats. There are birding dogs, sheepherding dogs, search-and-rescue dogs. There are those massive and beautiful sled dogs that will sacrifice their own well-being to pull you through blizzards to safety in Arctic snowstorms. It even seems to make them happy to meet the challenge and bring you through to safety.

Most times when people share their "dogs are better" lists, they often end with, a dog is your very best friend.

This list of dog qualities also mentions their frequent love of work. The canine who relishes a good walk or run, leaping and catching a freebie in their teeth, or repeatedly fetching a stick thrown in the lake is expressing a love for industry that is not found in the average feline.

Cats can be quiet and alone. They do not need to work to save your life through the worst blizzard. Unless they have been harmed in some way, they are not edgy or shouty. They know their own mind and express their own will. Just try training your cat to do some of those immensely useful things. You may call them by name, but do they come bounding up to you in response? They will come when they want to come.

The person comparing the two creatures will conclude that cats must not, then, care or be interested in your well-being. They care only about themselves. In summary, those people say with some kind of triumph, you can't count on a cat.

I am glad that people find love and friendship in a dog companion. I have done so, too, and still feel the loss of our beloved dog, Max. But I find a deep companionship of a different kind—which is also full of love and friendship—in Martin and Rosa.

I admit that there is something different about the relationship I have with my cats from that which I have had with dogs. For starters, it is true, my cats rarely come when I call. And yes, they do leave my side, all the time and pretty much whenever they desire. They don't perform tricks or look to please me in ways that Max used to do so well. Cats retain something a little bit wild. Domesticated, they always remain somewhat untamed.

I think this is the crux of why some people don't like them. They're reminded every time they look into a cat's eyes; it makes some people uncomfortable. Their pupils are able to contract into those tiny slits. And sometimes they don't look away. They stare. And they possess a third eyelid.

There are the sounds cats make too, confirming prejudices that people have. For example, the sound of a cat's cries has long been associated with demonic possession. When a cat is harmed by another animal or hurt in some way, they will scream and shriek—it can be earsplitting, the pain you hear in their voices. Dogs, in similar circumstances, often moan and whimper in ways that are humanlike. We sympathize with what reminds us of ourselves.

Most dogs have willing, obedient, completely tamed eyes. When Max had to be put down (his stomach was in knots from something he'd eaten, and surgery was too dangerous), my wife and I looked into those eyes, and we cried.

Martin and Rosa's eyes are different. They are not similar to human ones. They remain a bit mysterious. They are not fully tame, and they are not waiting to agree to whatever we ask of them. It's something I love about them. Martin's eyes are intense, or at least they sometimes can be. At times he will glare, his ears go pointed, and his pupils fill with black opals, surrounded by green, as his eyes communicate pointedly—not pleadingly, never begging—that I must *pay attention to this now.*

As I mentioned, Francis of Assisi understood and appreciated this wildness in creatures, preferring animals remain in their wild form rather than being domesticated. In fact, he became famous for purchasing caged birds in order to set them free. "Why did you allow someone to capture you?" he once asked them before letting them go. If he was given a live rabbit for the friars to prepare a meal, he would set it free. There's even a well-known story of him talking with a wolf, asking it not to hurt anyone, even as Francis respected the wolf's right to roam wild and free.

A bit untamed himself, Saint Francis began a spiritual movement around the same time Saint Dominic formed the Dominican Order. But it is striking how differently he and Dominic responded to religious authority. Francis mostly took a hands-off approach, as in, "Let's do our best to keep religious heirarchy's hands off of what we are trying to do." Dominic, on the other hand, frequently visited Rome, asking for permission and seeking the approval of bishops, Curia, and the pope.

Francis was untamed in other ways as well. He didn't join a monastery, for instance, and didn't start one. He didn't like the wealth that monasteries then represented or the security they offered. He preferred instead the vulnerability of sleeping outdoors or in caves or in borrowed places. In the early days of his spiritual movement, for example, Francis often slept in churches, like an undocumented immigrant might do today, as a place of sanctuary from the authorities.

Maybe you've heard of the seventeenth-century Japanese Zen poet, Matsuo Bashō? Deeply spiritual, doggedly individual, he too was more like a cat than a dog. A crafter of beautiful haiku, Bashō once said:

> Do not follow
> in the footsteps
> of the ancient ones.
> Seek what they sought.

There's a difference between obedience that quietly follows along and faithfulness that finds a unique path. The latter tends to be much more catlike.

One of my favorite cats ever was Bowie-hena. She came to us with a Hebrew name. We adopted her when her humans were leaving Vermont to move to Pennsylvania. One of Bowie's humans was Larry, who worked with me in the little publishing house in Woodstock, Vermont, that I co-ran at that time. I said to Larry, of course I would love to take her.

We lived in a log cabin on a hillside of twenty acres of pine and oak. It was rustic, to say the least. There were also large owls, fisher cats, and the sound of wolves at night. Bowie came to us declawed—something I would never do to a cat—in fact, no one ever should. Those who would harm a cat to protect their furniture might consider a hamster or a goldfish instead. Cats need their claws to be safe, to feel safe, and to be healthy emotionally and physically. Bowie's humans told us she'd never been let outdoors before. So the first thing Bowie did when she arrived was bolt out the door the second it was left open wide enough for her slim body. We all ran into the woods to find her and bring her back to safety. I was terrified, imagining that she would either not find her way back or be attacked by something, or both. We all bushwhacked the undergrowth and cornered Bowie successfully. I grabbed her up in my arms and put her back inside.

A few hours later, this happened again when someone happened to come to the door. Again, we all ran into the woods looking for her and screaming after her. I think it took four of us to catch her again and take put her back inside. The next day, this happened again. And then again the day after that. Finally we started to figure it out. I said, "Claws or no claws, owls or no owls, this cat was born to be outside. I don't think there is anything we can really do about it. This is who she is." It turns out that Bowie-hena means, in Hebrew, "Come here." Larry, a Hebrew speaker, knew what he was doing when he named her.

That cat lived another decade moving rather freely in and out of the front door to our cabin, roaming those woods, and returning hours later. She was fifteen by the time she stopped desiring to go outside every day (fifteen years of age to a domesticated cat is about the same as seventy-five to you and me), before she "retired" to being an all-indoors cat.

Her coming and going was not an ideal situation. I was conflicted with her desire to be a community cat and knowing she would kill small animals and birds from instinct "in the wild," while cheerfully gobbling kibble from a bowl in the warm kitchen. Bowie was rarely so quick as to snatch chickadees out of the air, but many a vole and small rodent met its death somewhere in those woods, as evidenced by "gifts" left on our front porch. I am sorry for that. That's also the reason why the ancient Egyptians domesticated cats and then prized them so highly.

In our own spirituality, we might learn to appreciate and respect what is wild and unknown—like a cat—in ourselves and in other creatures. We learn to better love the mystery presence that is in each of us, and in other creatures, when we embrace that untamed quality. Too often we think highly of ourselves and our capacities and what we can keep in our "control," and too little do we consider the wildness of other creatures. Many justify this approach by taking a line from the book of Genesis where God tells Adam and Eve that they are to have dominion over the other creatures. What problems that wrongful interpretation has caused.

Michel de Montaigne, the Renaissance writer, was the first modern thinker to question this attitude. In his longest essay, he wrote, "Is it possible to imagine anything more ridiculous than that this miserable and puny creature, who is not so much as master of himself, exposed to shocks on all sides, should call himself Master and Emperor of the universe?" He goes on to say how arrogant it is of us to assume that we're "the only creature in this great edifice that has the capacity to know the beauty and the several parts of it, the only one who is able to give thanks to the architect." Montaigne continues to reflect on the capacity of other creatures, and then, in particular, his own cat. Several paragraphs later he muses, "When I play with my cat, who knows but that she regards me more as a plaything than I do her?"

We so want to understand it all and to believe that we see clearly into our relationships and ourselves. There was a book published more than two decades ago in which its author believed she had discovered and delineated the language of Cat—*How to Speak Cat: The Essential Primer of Cat Language*. The author wrote about personal pronouns, having found two sets, "those for use by Cats and those for 'non-Cats.'"

Sometimes we claim too much and try too hard. We are motivated by love and passion for what we love, but sometimes a mystery—a wildness—is meant to be unsolved. I am reminded of the anecdote told in the apocryphal Gospel of Bartholomew (sometimes called "The Questions of Bartholomew"), where the apostles of Christ want to ask Mary how she carried "him who cannot be carried" and "gave birth to one of such great magnitude," but the group hesitates to ask such direct, personal questions. The great Peter and the beloved John refuse to do it, so Bartholomew volunteers to step forward. He boldly asks the question of Mary, and she responds: "Are you really asking me about this mystery? If I begin to tell you, fire will come forth from my mouth and set all the world ablaze."

To live with a spirituality that is mystery, that is wildness, is to honor that fire within ourselves, whether we are creaturely companions or human others. What we see in our cats' eyes—unique and ultimately inexplicable—is in us too. And it is good.

Cat and Human Practice

We need spiritual practices today that help us unlearn unhealthy, unthinking obedience. And to embrace the wildness that our cats know, that Saint Francis understood. For today, let me suggest a simple practice we can all do, wherever we are. I call this the "Spiritual Practice of Saying No." Try it.

Think for a moment of a situation in which you said yes in order to please someone else, even though you knew that you should have said no. Relive this situation again, now, in your imagination. What did it look like? How did you feel? Take your time exploring the scene. Now—put yourself in that situation again, in your imagination, and this time say no as you should have the first time. And feel the difference within yourself, where you said something because it came from you, not from guilt or a sense of people pleasing. (If applicable, you may even want to write a letter or send a text or make a phone call to, in fact, relive the opportunity, and this time say no.)

CHAPTER TWELVE

Don't Take Embarrassment Seriously

One afternoon, my wife and daughter and I were preparing dinner in the kitchen when water began to drip from the ceiling above. A drop landed on my head, which I began to ponder, and then a second later a drop landed on my daughter's head, and she said, "Where's that coming from?" We looked up and saw a rivulet pooled around the light fixture in the ceiling in the middle of the kitchen, and somehow my wife immediately knew what was happening. She left the room and ran upstairs. Sima and I followed her closely.

My daughter's room is immediately above the kitchen. What we saw when we got there was beyond anything I'd imagined. Sima's large fishbowl was on its side, on the floor, all of its water and contents pouring out, including Sima's goldfish, gently flapping its pectoral fins against the wood flooring.

Then we saw the scoundrel, Martin, crouching in the corner of the room. He had done what I suppose we could have imagined he would do, given the curiosity he'd been expressing lately around a certain sparkly, lively fish on Sima's desk.

Could Martin have plotted all the way to reason that, if he slowly pushed the heavy fishbowl off the desk, onto the floor, that fish would pop out of it, becoming available to a hungry cat? I doubt this, but the idea intrigues me still. The truth is, when the fishbowl hit the floor and caused a mild disaster in our house, the fish *did* pop out and was flapping in front of Martin's eyes. But then the moment he saw the three of us run into that room, Martin ran out. We didn't see him again for at least two hours. Which was fine. We had cleanup to do, and a goldfish to rehabilitate.

(A similar scenario played out, as this book was going to press, involving my daughter's two gerbils, involving Olive being deftly grabbed at the last moment out of Martin's open mouth, but that'll be a story for another day.)

No doubt there's a cleverness to a domesticated cat that's unique among animals we humans choose to live with. Martin reminds us of that all the time. Such qualities, combined with those unique, intense feline eyes I mentioned earlier, are also, I suspect, why cats are rarely portrayed personably in fairy tales. Think of the tales you have read or had read to you. In all of them, almost invariably the cat is the creature bearing down upon something smaller than itself. The cat is the one most likely possessed of wordless, thoughtless, evil intent, and its would-be prey is usually, in contrast, the most thoughtful and humanlike mouse, rabbit, bird, or goldfish.

I grew up on Tom and Jerry cartoons and E. B. White's *Stuart Little*. The mouse was always the parent or sibling or aunt or uncle or child, while the cat was a malevolent solitary living somewhere deep inside a wall. The mouse often even wore human clothes, drove a car, and spoke perfect English. From the stories of Jacob and Wilhelm Grimm to Italian and Scandinavian folktales, our human imaginations have turned cats into ominous beasts. This is perhaps why, when I once said something praiseworthy about my cats on Twitter, a friend responded with, "I think our cats would eat us, if they felt they could get away with it."

As one example of this, consider the Grimms' tale, "Cat and Mouse in Partnership," which is number two of one hundred and thirty-nine in *The Complete Grimm's Fairy Tales* on my shelf, with commentary by Joseph Campbell. It is a short story of a cat and mouse who agree to make a house together and share their food and supplies. But the cat lies to the mouse repeatedly, going out by himself frequently and while away from home gobbling up what had been promised to be shared with the mouse. In the end, when the mouse accuses the cat of his selfish deeds, the story ends with "scarcely had she spoken it before the cat sprang on her, seized her, and swallowed her down. Verily, that is the way of the world."

But that is not the way of the world. I don't think it is even the way of cats.

A cat will lick a paw when she is embarrassed. Or she will lick her face. A second later, she will run back into the fray to play some more. Psychologists call these behaviors "displacement activities," and they are one of the many behaviors that we have in common with our feline friends. A couple hours after our goldfish bowl fiasco, I watched as Martin strolled back into the living room, where we were all gathered, hopped up onto the couch, and licked his face.

We humans aren't so dissimilar. Consider, for instance, what you do when you feel confused. Do you scratch your head? Do you look away, perhaps downward and to the left or right? It is not as if these routines have taught you that answers come after scratching your scalp or diverting your eyes. These are not behaviors we have learned as effective tools for realization but are more like gestures of coping, pausing, reconsidering, maybe even avoidance. Cats have these anxious tics, too, to deal with mild embarrassments.

Martin and Rosa groom themselves when they feel awkward or foolish. To lick a paw and apply it to your face a few times in rapid succession is sometimes a sign that you're in mild recovery mode or simply unsure of what to do next.

I sometimes wonder about the various devices for determining human personality types and how these might apply to felines. I think of this each time I talk with Martin and watch his facial expressions. All cats have facial muscles that work what we call eyebrows on humans, and Martin is one of those cats who has long whiskers in those eyebrow places. They often bob up and down as I talk. Earlier, I suggested that one day I might consider applying the Enneagram to Martin and Rosa; well, that time is now. I can't resist.

We all have our ways of dealing with anxiety, embarrassment, and moments of feeling awkward and unsure. I remember once, decades ago, when I had an unpredictable rageaholic for a boss, that there was a certain pair of shoes which, when I wore them, I felt just a tiny bit more confident in myself—and when I had a hunch that a day at the office would be tougher than usual, I would wear those shoes. I look back on those times now and wince, thinking how good it would have been if I could have taken stronger remedies to the problem. Why didn't I just quit the job and find another? But I did what I thought I could do or had to do.

Martin, I think, is probably an Enneagram Eight. An Eight often has had a difficult childhood and becomes "tough" as a result. Eights are confident, assertive, sometimes confrontational, and occasionally heroic. Perhaps something happened in those first two months that left little Martin feeling he had to compensate for some litter pain and disappointment. In one of his books on the Enneagram, Ian Cron explains an Eight like this:

> Many Eights bury the painful feelings of their pasts and create a tough persona capable of withstanding anything life dishes out. Some overcome problems at home by being leaders at school, getting kudos for their grit and determination. Many Eight children are driven, but it's not quite the same way that other types are driven: it's not to be admired for their success (like Threes) or to satisfy an inner perfectionism (like Ones). Rather, Eights believe they need to be large and in charge. They tell themselves that they must conquer the world before it turns on them and disintegrates into the chaos they often experienced in their childhood.

Perhaps it is odd to identify possible childhood diffi-culties in Martin, since he joined us at the age of three months, but three months to a kitten is similar to the first eighteen months in human development. A lot can happen.

Martin's sister Rosa, meanwhile, is perhaps an Enneagram Nine. Where Eights are called Challengers, Nines are usually called Peacemakers. A Nine is easy going and self-effacing. A Nine does not make demands but rather finds ways of agreement. They are optimistic creatures, and supportive, but can also become complacent and avoidant. Ian Cron says this about the Enneagram Nine:

> Nines are usually the low-maintenance kids every parent wants. They've been called the "sweethearts of the Enneagram" and can often showcase the best qualities of the other eight types, merging with the priorities and opinions of other people in order to avoid conflict. Nines intuitively seem to know how to read other people and adapt accordingly.

My friends will tell you that this is how I have often described Rosa: She's a sweetheart. She's the easy stability and peace of mind to Martin's frequently challenging little Napoleon. She is the sweetest cat I have ever had.

The unfolding of a human being happens through small failures like everyday embarrassments. Cats show us how to do this. Experts explain that displacement activities can become a serious problem when they turn into obsessive disorders—"psychogenic alopecia," they call it, and I don't really know what that means. But those casual moments of out-of-context licking and grooming have the potential to grow, if stress is great and solutions few, into plucking out patches of one's fur. If this is happening, the message to the cat owner is the same as to the human for whom displacement activities may become obsessive: Find a professional to guide you through.

The Catholic patron saint of embarrassment is the little-known Wiborada, a ninth-century Swiss nun. Skilled in Latin prayers and theological texts, Wiborada was accused of some wrongdoing—we don't know precisely what. And as sometimes happened, her sentence was "ordeal by fire," which meant that she was forced to walk on hot coals over a short distance and not only survive but demonstrate very little injury. She apparently succeeded on all counts, but it is said that the embarrassment of whatever it was that she had done, or not done, wounded her so much that she left the convent to become a hermit, or "anchoress." Gifts of prophecy and other miracles then followed the anchoress like swallows, to the amazement of everyone.

The lesson that a Catholic is supposed to take from this kind of saintly anecdote is that there is a holy person who came before us to whom we might appeal for help from heaven when we, too, face similar difficulties. That's one lesson, maybe, but I think more of Martin push, push, pushing that fishbowl onto the floor, licking his lips at the sight of the flopping goldfish, getting caught in the act, fleeing to another room, and then resurfacing two hours later, rather nonchalantly, onto the couch beside me, with an only slightly anxious paw to his face. He recovered very nicely. We moved on. This is just another way in which I am convinced that there is a part of us that unfolds only in creaturely lessons when we truly encounter and learn from another animal.

Practice What Cats Do

In chapter 4 we looked at a practice I'd like to return to, appropriate for this chapter. This is a spiritual skill that is too uncommon today: Make yourself foolish somehow today. Perhaps look into the religious tradition—in Buddhism, Catholicism, and Eastern Orthodoxy, in particular—of "holy fools" and the ways that they show disdain for the world's ways of power by pursuing something entirely different. Perhaps it's to look at your cat, the running out the door, the avoidance grooming, and how they rather easily find a way back to peaceful kingdom.

Practice embarrassment so as to take it less seriously. It is important to do your silly, weird, sheepish, sideways thing in a way that does not add more positive attention to you in the process. For example, you wouldn't be practicing true foolishness by wearing a goofy hat; the hat would probably only add to your reputation or image as a fun person. The purpose here is to lead people to questioning you just a bit. Why is his hair all a mess? Why is she sitting on the sidewalk? And then find your catlike balance again.

CHAPTER THIRTEEN

See into Things

If you have cat companions, you've noticed the intensity with which they can focus attention on you. Definitely before mealtimes, and certainly at those times when they would like to be touched. They follow you with their eyes; they look into your eyes; they rub against you; they sit on top of whatever it is you are attempting to do at that moment that isn't about them. They do all they can to communicate with us.

Martin, as I mentioned in an earlier chapter, when he's hungry begins to eat the lampshades in our living room. Also when he's hungry and I am working, Martin hops on my desk and tries to stare me down. If that does not work, he begins to poke me, or knock things over on the shelves behind me. He knocks over the same things, over and over, each time. He knows that I will then wake up and realize: Hey, this is Martin, and he needs something! Rosa will do likewise, in fact, as I type this, she is laying across both of my arms as I try to tap the computer keys. If my eyes remain on the screen for too long, she reaches a paw in the air to get my attention. Look at me!

We want to know what they think. What is going on in their minds? Do they think about us? What do they know of us—our habits, our routines, perhaps too our inconsistencies and emotions, when these seem to cause some noticeable disruption in the household routines?

While we've heard stories about dogs so in tune with their owners as to sense an illness in them or see some danger approaching them, we know cats do this too. It's less common and less obvious, partially because it's less common for cats to be at their humans' side, come when they call, and overtly reveal their emotions. But cats have a heightened sense of smell and often know when there has been a chemical or hormonal change inside their humans. For instance, there was Oscar, a cat resident of a nursing home in Providence, Rhode Island, two decades ago, whose story was written up in the *New England Journal of Medicine*. Nursing home employees began to notice that Oscar, who roamed the facility as a care animal, ended up favoring certain residents with his time and attention—residents who were profoundly ill and soon after died. A bit of investigation showed that Oscar was jumping up onto the beds of those who he somehow understood to be near death and sitting with them in their last days and moments. Oscar had that feline quality of special olfactory intuition, and he probably also was attentive to the faces of humans, and the subtle changes on them, in life's last moments.

There are also anecdotes of cats sensing high blood pressure in humans, coming to their aid, and purring. Cats have also been said to detect cancer, as dogs have done, by smell. Oncologists have confirmed that cancer does in fact have a smell, confirmed in articles in several medical journals.

Cats also have been known to protect their humans from calamities. I think first of the cat in Japan who was the subject of a video gone viral a few years ago. The cat, caught on a nanny cam, jumped from a chair when she saw her toddler crawling toward the edge of a flight of stairs. As the child teetered in that dangerous direction, the cat got in front of the child and pushed her over and over again, first gently, then intently, until the toddler gave up on trying to get any closer to the stairwell. (Yes, one wonders: *Where was the nanny!*)

They don't only look closely and intently at us when they are hungry. Our cats are often observant in ways that we rarely are. They see something and focus on it with sustained attention, watching for changes, sometimes twitching with anticipation of the next very slight movement. I marvel at what they can see—especially because I know that their eyesight is not as good as ours. Cats are more nearsighted than us, and they can't see color as well as we can. They see slightly better than we do at nighttime—the tapetum lucidum, a thin layer of tissue behind the retina, is like a mirror that reflects light in a cat's eyes. This is why when you shine light into the eyes of your cats at night, they glow eerily. But during the daytime their eyesight is almost ten times worse than ours. All the more reason why I'm curious to see them watching birds and squirrels outside the windows, or a ladybug on the opposite side of the glass—they notice details I do not and remain focused on things long after I have moved on.

My vision—both eyesight and insight—tends to be scattered. I bop from one thing to another, forgetting what I saw a minute ago, my attention span like a gnat without a lightbulb. So I look to teachers like Thich Nhat Hanh, who spent much of his teaching on the subject of cultivating attention. I remember one of his talks in Vermont. He spent five minutes on how to pay attention to what's happening in you, through you, to you, on the toilet. I chuckled about it then, and I'm not going to talk about that now because I promise you, I've found no spiritual lessons from Martin and Rosa relating to their cat box. However, ever since I heard that talk, I have been trying to develop my own skills of attention. There is a way of seeing things, and then there is a way of seeing *into* things.

Thay used to say: "When we learn to calm our minds in order to look deeply at the true nature of things, we can arrive at full understanding, which dissolves every sorrow and anxiety and gives rise to acceptance and love."

Most of my life I did a poor job of giving attention to the world around me, to the people in my life, to the Spirit that's trying to inspire me. I'm not alone. A lot of people have trouble with this. It wasn't until my forties that there was a change. The mystics of many religious traditions say this too—it takes maturity and age to be able to begin to see into things. I couldn't, and still can't, see deeply without first allowing my responsibilities and my desire to achieve (which was so strong in me in young adulthood) to fall away.

In what has long been my favorite of all the Wendell Berry *Sabbath Poems*, the opening line of one from 1979 has the poet going among trees to "sit still." Then and there, the poet says, "All my stirring becomes quiet." And only then does he begin to see clearly. You can't focus on proving your worth and personal achievement and still truly look deeply at the true nature of things. Something has to be let go.

Likewise, something has to go, be understood to believe (and by believing, I mean, live as if) what the poet Mary Oliver so simply and beautifully expresses,

it is a serious thing / just to be alive

I envy the cats in my house who are not trying to impress me or each other and who can see the world with simple intensity—just being alive. Without blinking, they can focus on small details and take them in, and then they can just as easily and freely go back to sleeping or purring. They cause me to stop and look, too—sometimes at them, and more often at the details of my life that would otherwise pass me by. When I was in my twenties and thirties, I excused myself from seeing into things, saying that I didn't have the time. There was too much to do. Now I hope it's not too late to turn. I want that kind of attention, that kind of freedom, where "all my stirring becomes quiet."

Human Practice

Our practice this time—both for you and others around you, is borrowed from Annie Dillard's 1974 classic book of essays, *Pilgrim at Tinker Creek*:

> When I was six or seven years old, growing up in Pittsburgh, I used to take a precious penny of my own and hide it for someone else to find. It was a curious compulsion; sadly, I've never been seized by it since. For some reason I always "hid" the penny along the same stretch of sidewalk up the street. I would cradle it at the roots of

a sycamore, say, or in a hole left by a chipped-off piece of sidewalk. Then I would take a piece of chalk, and, starting at either end of the block, draw huge arrows leading up to the penny from both directions. After I learned to write I labeled the arrows: SURPRISE AHEAD or MONEY THIS WAY.

She would leave the penny, with hints of where to find it, believing that someone would come by and look closely, and then be delighted at their discovery. She adds: "There are lots of things to see. . . . The world is fairly studded and strewn with pennies cast broadside from a generous hand. But—and this is the point—who gets excited by a mere penny?"

For this practice consider how might you leave some anonymous clue to even a small shiny good in the world today for people who are in need of awe, wonder, and discovery. Be creative.

CHAPTER FOURTEEN

Know That You Are Loved

In the pandemic I became more attentive to my surroundings, and also angrier. I suspect that these two factors have worked like cause and effect. My initial response to change is not often positive, so that worked against me for starters. Then came all of the changes wrought by the pandemic itself—sequestering, illness, death of friends, immobility, claustrophobia. But in that time and through that time, I thanked God for Martin and Rosa.

They helped during these difficult years. They showed me the clearer way to gratitude upon awaking in the morning, for having loved ones nearby, about feeling the sunshine on my skin—even when I could not get out and walk in it as I once did, for seeing birds with pleasure and hearing birdsong with attentiveness and learning to communicate better with my eyes from behind what became ubiquitous pandemic masks.

A love is rooted in the ground beneath our feet and surrounds us like the wind and sky. There's nothing we do to earn this—it is part of understanding our creatureliness—and my cats remind me of this too. So does the Muscogee Creek Nation poet Joy Harjo. In her latest memoir, she tells this story:

> There was a Navajo woman who lived far out on the reservation in a *hogan*, the traditional home of the indigenous people there. She was of a righteous nature, still prayed in the morning with cornmeal, took care of her sheep, and was loved and well-respected by her neighbors. She was also blind. She was visited one day by the Holy Ones. As her *hogan* filled with the powerful presence of sacredness, the Holy Ones told her, as they towered over her, that they came to give a warning to the people.

We are nearing times where we will experience earth changes, famine, and strife, because people are forgetting their original teachings.

We are in those times now. Maybe by the time you read this, we will have learned how to be human.

To learn to be human, to locate your gratitude in this love—and to discover new ways of earth care—you might try waking before the sunrise and allowing your thankfulness to rise with the day, "to remember the original teachings." When I do this, it is rarely without a cat nearby. The creatures of the earth accompany me. They are always awake before me, or else they appear suddenly when I emerge from the bedroom. Rosa greets me with an expression that almost seems to be an imitation of human talking. Looking up at my face, and while nodding her head, Rosa says something like, "Hmmmf."

So I "hmmmf" back, imagining that it helps her know how her attempt to communicate with me was entirely successful.

Our cats like to talk with us if we have the patience to listen and respond. So go the rest of the creatures and the earth itself. Whether or not we "completely" understand their language, they seem to appreciate the attempts. After two years of building this practice, Rosa and I can sustain several expressions of back-and-forth verbal exchange, our eyes remaining on each other.

Sometimes it's not always an exchange. Our cats like to listen when we talk. They are sensitive to noise and sound. This is why they will find a napping spot far from the crying child in the bedroom or away from the dog that barks in the apartment next door. Rosa, for instance, will enjoy my daughter's company in her room, but not when the gerbils take to their wheel to noisy effect. It is then that Rosa darts away. But all cats enjoy the sound of their humans' voices when they are gentle and speaking and not raised. The everyday voices of the household.

In the evenings when we are in the living room, there Rosa and Martin often will sit. For instance, since my wife is a rabbi, we have a weekly Torah study on Saturday mornings in a downstairs room facing the street. There sits Martin, always, either on a chair or on the center rug, first listening, then falling asleep, among the gathered singing and talking people. This is also why, as many a cat owner will attest, if a quiet afternoon at home is interrupted with a phone call, our cats will sometimes show an inordinate interest in rubbing against us while we answer it. Kitty likes to hear us talk, and she may be assuming at those moments, which suddenly punctuate the quiet, that we are surely talking to her. (Or that we should, instead, be talking to her!) This is why I have developed a spiritual practice of talking with my cats.

I have also learned to touch them affectionately, as touching them is a way of expressing and receiving love. As we discussed earlier, their purring is a gesture of contentedness, at least, and perhaps even affection and love. Martin will rub up against my legs, purring, asking to be petted. How I love to be wanted like this! I give him the attention he wants, and my love at those moments is not selfless; his purring and desire, even the look on his whiskered face, tells me that I am the love he needs at that moment. I am his conduit to the love that surrounds us. It is mutual.

Oftentimes, I will lift Martin to my shoulder and hold him there with one arm. He straddles my left scapula like a saddle and seems to feel quite comfortable in that position for several minutes. We walk around the house that way. I think he likes to sit there like a prince, and I like to hear his purring even closer to my ear. I talk while we walk. He purrs and nestles against my neck, which are his ways of communicating with me. Then, sometimes, I will hold him to my chest for a minute to feel his purr like a heartbeat on my own.

What is this if not a form of mysticism?

I have a deep, informing sense of God's presence in my life, rooted in feelings of grace, love, and gratitude that rarely seems like it needs to be explained or spoken out loud. These mystical feelings are not ecstatic, and they don't give rise to special visions or private messages. But they fill me in a way that, I hope, results in my expressing grace, love, and gratitude to others through my actions in the world.

In the preface to this book, I mentioned one example of how I have occasionally found easier happiness with my cats than with my children; their devotion tends to be unquestioning. Then, in one of the chapters, I spoke of something that many cat lovers will easily understand as well—how we are often able to grasp their love, and fulfill it to their satisfaction, better than we can for the humans who are also our loved ones. Here is one final example of the same thing: My cats' fealty to me does not fade as they approach adulthood. Their attachment to me does not ebb and flow as a human's does for their parents in a developmental way. I have often said, after a beer or two, talking with fellow parents of teenagers, "If you think about it, our job is to make ourselves irrelevant in their lives. If we raise them well, they come to leave us almost entirely behind. They don't need us anymore. Sometimes that feels rewarding. Other times, it feels like, *What was the point of it all?*"

With my cats, it is different. Martin is resting on my outstretched legs now as I type this. He is already the equivalent in age to a sixteen-year-old boy. My son, Joe, was mostly disinterested in me by the time he reached that age. His world became his friends and his growing ambition to find his own voice and way in this world. He was becoming a man, and his attachment to me flowed. Martin's won't. I realize that Martin leans on me like this probably for reasons most easily answered biologically, or about learned behavior. In other words, I feed him and I stroke him, so I am the replacement for his mother who first fed him and loved him into existence. That is just fine with me. I signed up for this job, I love it, and the relationship feeds me too. Unlike my human children, my cats don't grow up to know better. Martin and I will be this way until he is old, even older than me.

A dog will often look at you with faithfulness, but a cat you are stroking looks at you with love. Rosa and I will especially look at each other this way, knowing well that the other is filling us with affection.

A recent study from Claremont Graduate University in California by Professor Paul Zak has in fact discovered that cats (and dogs too) release a hormone called oxytocin when they interact with each other, and when they are interacting with humans who care for them. This feel-good hormone is produced in the brains of humans too, for instance, when lovers have sex, or when a mother is holding her baby. Increased levels of the hormone cause us to then become even more loving, more compassionate. Oxytocin has "behavioral effects," Zak explained from his study. Both humans and cats have increased levels of oxytocin when they are together lovingly. Zak concluded, in his 2014 article in *The Atlantic*, that these actual physiological changes in us help explain the depths to which our attachments can go when we bond with an animal. For instance, in case you needed a scientific explanation for the degree of your affection for your animal companions, he wrote: "Oxytocin might explain why people spend thousands of dollars to treat a pet medically rather than euthanize it and simply get a new animal."

We are all filled with love and adoration, not only for each other but for the world. This is good. May it increase in our brains and in our lives. It is who we are, and it precedes everything else.

There are rare occasions, however, when Rosa's cat-ness collides with my humanness, and after sustained stroking of her body, she will begin to bite, just a bit, and claw, just a bit, because for her this is an extension of her pleasure and her love. I'll end up with a claw mark, even perhaps a blood spot on a wrist if I don't let her go quickly. We sometimes have to let the other go.

But the love that sustains us all remains. I hope that you know this, with or without a cat beside you.

I won't for a minute pretend or suggest that we all have the same opportunities in life to experience love and its related effects. Nor that we all grow up in families that nurture us, with parents who do their best to carry us into the world to succeed and be happy. The inequalities of life are staggering. But I do suggest that we are loved equally by God, by holy mystery, by the Spirit of all that creates and sustains and reaches out to know us and lift us up. The earth loves us all equally too. I hope that you know you are loved by these mysteries. You are. I hope you know this, just as Rosa knows that she is loved by me.

Human Practice

Try looking at someone the way your cat looks at you with affection. You can't do this successfully as an affect. You have to mean it. And you will probably not mean a look of love for another creature or person without also accessing the love that is inside you. Then, you will not only be better for others but you will be prepared to experience the beauty of the world. As the late Desmond Tutu said:

> We were made to enjoy music, to enjoy beautiful sunsets, to enjoy looking at the billows of the sea and to be thrilled with a rose that is bedecked with dew. . . . Human beings are actually created for the transcendent, for the sublime, for the beautiful, for the truthful . . . and all of us are given the task of trying to make this world a little more hospitable to these beautiful things.

CHAPTER FIFTEEN

Be Persistent and Thankful

A recent study by Samuel Perry, a professor of sociology at the University of Oklahoma, published in the *Journal for the Scientific Study of Religion*, suggests that having a cat as a companion is, for many people, a kind of "God substitute."

Perry finds a sympatico relationship between cat behavior, human behavior around cats, and what we tend to look for in a God. He writes: "[Cats] want to interact with you but it's always on their terms and it's always about them. We want to always win their affections and it bothers us when we think they might be somehow displeased with us. Cats are very godlike in those characteristics." The problems with this, however, are various. First of all, the researcher's conclusions are based on assumptions and a perpetuation of myths about cats, as well as myths about how most spiritual and religious people in fact relate to God. Perry's study is based on a lowest-common-denominator understanding of both.

It is true that, for some of us, a warm friend on the lap replaces the need for gathering in religious community and participating in religious observances the ways that others might do. But more often, for cat lovers who also consciously and sometimes passionately relate to God or seek after the divine, a cat reminds us that we are creatures, not gods, and teaches us to care for the creation of the God we seek and find. And the first and easiest way to express these things is with thankfulness. This is something I do upon waking, as my religious tradition teaches.

It can be difficult under any circumstances to wake up and greet the day with hope. I almost always do, but I realized long ago that this is not my virtue but rather my disposition. "O sing to the Lord a new song; sing to the Lord, all the earth" (Ps. 96:1). I usually feel it, though I know others struggle in the morning. Many years ago, when my wife and

I were first together, for weeks, each morning, I would be walking happily around the house, talking, and looking at her somewhat confused and saying things like, "How are you?" And then, "What's wrong?" Finally, one morning she looked back at me and yelled, "Stop being so happy in the morning!"

We realized then that our mood trajectories go in reverse order from one another. I tend to wake up an optimist; she doesn't. When I am sad, it is often at the end of the day, when I am feeling worn out. She, in contrast, usually feels great by bedtime, having warmed up during the day, spending it doing many good and productive things.

During the pandemic, even people who were used to being "morning people," waking up with energy and focus, faced a fresh challenge. This happened for me. But I think we are supposed to wake up alive, with all the vigor and determination we can muster, every day, until we die. Martin and Rosa lead me. Whether that begins for you each day upon waking or culminates for you each evening by bedtime, it doesn't matter. Bring your muster.

All the spiritual practices we have done together so far have been designed as exercises to develop our catlike qualities: Surrendering, loving, living with discipline, playing, expanding our vision, paying closer attention to the world around us, pouncing. But the muscle that flexes all of these good habits or virtues—call them what you like—is the muscle of persistence. And persistence may be the most catlike spiritual quality of them all.

Martin will sometimes practice persistence while I am trying to write at my desk by lying all over the papers and books spread out there. He will sprawl onto his back, his head on my open laptop, as if to say, "*Look at me* rather than that glaring machine." Rosa is gentler but no less persistent. She wants to hop onto my lap once or twice each day for about three minutes of loving. During this special time, if I begin to look at my laptop, because we're sitting at my desk, she may even lift a paw to my chin, to guide my gaze back to her. I am serious. She has done this many times. It's adorable.

The Lakota medicine man and Catholic catechist Nicholas Black Elk lived a century ago, and he said, "It is in the darkness of their eyes that [people] get lost." He was referring to how we lose our vision and inspiration in times of trial or suffering. Our eyes dim, not just metaphorically, but we can no longer see our way clearly.

Becoming lost is rarely something that happens to us while on the road. In fact, with GPS, this is truer than Black Elk ever could have imagined. But I don't think he was talking about that kind of getting lost. Finding our way home or finding our way to where we need to go is no longer a matter of directions. Directions are easy and following them is easy. The problem is in the darkness of our eyes.

We are dispirited, and not just for a short while but sometimes day after day. People can see it in us. Perhaps you see it yourself, in your eyes, when you look in the mirror in the morning or at night. Even persistence—as in will power—is not enough. But I think if we combine it with necessary and regular gratitude, we will find our way home, practicing being thankful for the most basic things.

John Gray is the renowned philosopher who recently published a book about cats that I mentioned earlier. When *Feline Philosophy* came out, I bought it and read it right away, even though I found myself disagreeing with much that's in it. But some of his wisdom, when Gray offers advice that a cat might have for human beings, I took with me:

> Life is not a story. If you think of your life as a story, you will be tempted to write it to the end. But you do not know how your life will end, or what will happen before it does. It would be better to throw the script away. The unwritten life is more worth living than any story you can invent.

In this too, Martin and Rosa lead me. Humans wake up in the morning and want to know what the end of the day will feel like. We want to know where we are going and how we will get there. But when we do that—and we always seem to do that—we easily get lost. It is in our own eyes—in our own spirit—that we become lost.

The Christian mystic Julian of Norwich famously said in a quote I adapt here: "Turning away from God is Behovely, but All shall be well, and All manner of thing shall be well."

That Middle English word—*behovely*—means "necessary" or "useful." Turning from God—turning away from the good—can be destructive and hurtful to others. According to Julian, that turning is not only what you may have done wrong but what has turned away what is hurtful and painful around you. All will be well. God turns all things to good.

Similarly, Meister Eckhart, one of my favorite mystics, talks about our lives often being spent chasing after illusions—things or ideas that are not real. We become lost in these unrealities, especially how we see God, and ourselves, in illusory ways. God is not in fact seen but can be nonetheless known, as growing within us, born like a child, to animate our lives in every way. But, Eckhart says, God works in and through us only as well as we cooperate. He compares this to the baking of bread:

> If you heat up an oven and put in it loaves of oats, barley, rye, and wheat, there is only one source of heat for the oven and yet it works differently in the different loaves. One of them turns into a fine loaf of bread; the second comes

out much rougher, and the others rougher still. The heat is not to blame for the difference, but the material, which is unequal. Likewise, God does not work the same way in each of our lives.

Be thankful, be persistent, and see. See that your life is tangled up already with holiness, and open yourself to what already is all around you. We can each become fine loaves of rich bread. Don't turn away, open your heart and see what's hidden inside, and then—like a cat with attentive thankfulness—look at others without the kind of darkness in your eyes that keeps you from seeing it in them too.

Cat and Human Practice

Persistence is not so much something you practice as it is something you prepare yourself for. The best thing we can do is to put ourselves in a healthy position each day so that we move through it with fresh determination to do the good.

We need spiritual practices for good sleep, for eating well, for a life of moderation, for a healthy sexuality of giving and receiving, for meditation or prayer that centers us night and morning, that will allow us to wake up alive each day.

And then there is gratitude. There is nothing more important for us to practice than this. Jewish tradition offers a series of "morning blessings" to be said upon waking. I don't say these every day, but I say them every Saturday, and they help open the day. Here's how they begin: "Blessed are you, Awakener, our God, life of all the worlds, who removes sleep from my eyes, and slumber from my eyelids." A blessing that later follows is, "Blessed are you, The Imageless, our God, life of all the worlds, who made me in your image."

And, as I write this, Rosa has come to my desk to sit with me and with you. Maybe she is blessing the day too in the early hours of the morning.

CHAPTER SIXTEEN

Quiet Yourself

Mystery is essential to both our spirituality and our biology. But there is a whole school of thought, increasingly so, that suggests otherwise. We want to know everything, and we believe that we can know everything, eventually, somehow. For cat people, this school of thought sometimes looks like our trying to understand our cats' wants and talking with them about it. I know professionals who market their services to teach cat speak, and cat language, to their clients.

There are books, among them *How to Speak Cat: The Essential Primer of Cat Language.* The author, Alexandra Sellers, is described on the book jacket as an expert in many languages—including Cat. An extensive Part One covers grammatical questions, starting with personal pronouns, the verb "to be," and class one verbs. There are also many discussions of tonality, and these cover topics such as "the flattery voice," "the fantasy voice," and "the offended voice." She identifies fifteen consonants in Cat, including four versions of our letter r. Her key to pronunciation in the front matter relies on the Roman alphabet, with regrets (for not having yet discovered an original Cat alphabet), and includes this:

r   simple English untrilled r, as in "brawl"

rr   trilled r. The nearest human equivalent of this sound is formed when the tongue flutters on the hard palate.

R   uvular r, as in French "tresor"

RR   heavily rolled uvular r

Perhaps you will read this and think, *Yes, I hear those in my cat, too!* Or, like me, you may feel that sometimes we are only imagining we understand our cats with guides like this.

I had a beloved professor in seminary who spoke occasionally of the ineffableness of God. He didn't go on at length on this subject because he knew how that would be ridiculous. But I remember him telling a story from when he had taught at Yale Divinity School and some students were walking with him out of a chapel service one sunny morning. One student said, "What a beautiful service!" And another, trying to impress the professor, said, "Yes, but only if we know enough to benefit from the Latin text." My professor remembered responding to them both with, "If you caught 'Laud,' then I think you have enough."

Unspoken ways of spirituality are increasingly more important to me than spoken ones, just as signs and gestures of affection are what most often bind me to my loved ones, especially my cats. There is, for instance, the ubiquitous cat headbutt, when our cats lean into us, gently and affectionately, to show you the bond that they feel with you. A recent UK study also revealed another way that people can exchange nonverbal affection with their feline companions:

> When your cat blinks gently at you, it's a sign that he feels affection and trust. . . . Why? All cats rely on their sense of sight to survive, so when they deliberately diminish it by closing their eyes, they're showing that they feel happy and safe. According to a recent study at the universities of Portsmouth and Sussex, you can communicate with your cat by doing the same thing. "Try

narrowing your eyes at them as you would in a relaxed smile, followed by closing your eyes at them as you would in a relaxed smile, followed by closing your eyes for a couple of seconds," said Karen McComb, an animal behaviorist who supervised the study. "You'll find they respond in the same way themselves and you can start a sort of conversation."

Perhaps this will open up new ways for human beings to communicate with the unspeakable and ineffable One as well. Maybe we should try narrowing our human eyes as we "look" at the divine.

Most every religious tradition speaks of a knowledge of God. Most speak of knowing God as a duty or a pursuit or a practice, or simply the result of faithfulness to the revealed expectations of God in that tradition. I wonder, however, if it really works that way. If there is a knowledge of God, it strikes me that it is most likely and most often entirely unpredictable.

Across the traditions, adepts will often say that knowledge of the divine comes through obedience to the commandments or the disciplines or the dharma. Maybe so. In subtle but significant contrast, the medieval mystic Bernard of Clairvaux believed there was knowledge of God that came only through relationship. It is love of God that yields knowledge of God, Bernard said. Mystics of every tradition have offered other correctives of a more basic, native, elementary, empirical experience of holiness and beauty—call it simply "awareness"—as that which is the essential understanding (not exactly knowledge) of God. Creator, perhaps. Sustainer, maybe. Or universal inspiration. The breath of all things.

Whether it is love or awareness that brings us closer to God, the cats in our homes help carry us there. I remember an instance many years ago when my son, Joe, was only ten years old. We had found a kitten for him a year earlier to add to the two cats already in our home on the advice of Joe's pediatrician. At the time Joe was having trouble expressing anger in healthy ways, including instances at school that resulted in my being called to the principal's office. We found a graceful and gentle kitten at the shelter and Joe named her Mia. She was immediately a calming effect upon his life. When Joe would become upset, which was almost daily, he learned to retreat to Mia and sometimes to his room with Mia, to calm down. He would hold her on his lap and she would purr and Joe would calm down.

There are many scientific studies to show that humans who live with cats have, on average, lower blood pressure than humans who do not.

Joe loved Mia intensely and needed her. But one day when he was more upset than usual, when he got to his room and slammed his door behind him, there was Mia looking up at him with those gentle eyes. Joe wanted nothing to do with being comforted at that moment, and when Mia jumped up onto his lap, he tossed her back down to the floor in anger. As Joe remembers and feels the pain of that troubling moment now, almost twenty years later, Mia quietly and persistently walked right back to his bedside, paused for only a second, and hopped back up. There she remained, and Joe calmed down.

There is a quietness that leads to the knowledge of spiritual things, and only being quiet will get you there.

Catlike Meditation Practice

Sometimes the best way to quiet ourselves is with slow, meditating breaths and slow, meditative body movements. One version of this practice comes from a recent book of meditations by the Buddhist teacher Willa Blythe Baker. She uses the practice for what she calls "Summoning Grace." For our purposes, I am pulling out its essence.

Baker's practice involves breathing deliberately and moving the hips deliberately while on the floor on all fours—like a cat. She advises "inhaling as your back sags and exhaling as it arches." I can attest: this feels good. Then, she writes: "Now begin to circle your hips. To help you get into the spirit of the movement, summon your inner feline (think cat, lion, tiger, cougar, jaguar, puma). Circle in a slow, leisurely way. . . . Move your head this way and that, looking back at your tail from one side and then the other." If you're like me, hopefully you can find a place and time to do this when you know you will be completely undisturbed. (Or add it to another practice from previous chapters of the "holy fool.")

When you feel done—"growl, roar, and shake your body all over, like a lion stepping from the river to the shore." Then, I would add, know that it is from this inner growl and coiling power that your inner quiet comes.

CHAPTER SEVENTEEN

Pounce Frequently

Cats are all about connection. The visual artist Candice Lin understands this. In a fall and winter 2021 exhibit at the Walker Art Center in Minneapolis, Lin's art centered on images and installations related to cats, inspired by her relationship with certain ones. She explained:

> I've always loved cats and had deep connection and communication with them. During this pandemic I had many months when I mainly interacted with my cat Roger. I think this time period stripped away everything that wasn't a source of necessity and soul-sustaining pleasure. Allowing myself to think about cats, and to make work centered around them, fed that need for comfort and connection that was scarce during this time.

Her cats-in-art included certain "cat demons," which resembled tomb-guardian statues in China, and a feline Qigong instructor on video repeat. She captured the vivacity of the feline spirit across cultures and throughout history.

Is it an accident that we rarely seem to see our cats feeling down in the dumps? Perhaps I misunderstand the signs, and when Martin and Rosa are lying still or walking around the house alone, they are, at times, depressed—but I don't think so. Hunt. Sleep. Play. Repeat. I think that's the way of life of felines everywhere, wild or domestic. They don't much trouble with troubles, which is part of why their companionship can be healing for those of us who do.

They live, instead, to pounce. In Ursula Le Guin's novella told by a cat, the cat hilariously admits: "It is not fun to hunt mice. It is exciting in an intense, terrible way. If there is a mouse, I cannot think of anything else. I cannot sleep. I cannot eat kibbles. I can only smell and hear and think of mouse. I don't understand this, and it makes me unhappy. . . . I always catch it. And then what? . . . It isn't to eat."

There is an intensity and passion for movement that sits deeply inside of a cat's psyche. In Medieval Christian art, some artists put a single cat in the corner or background of paintings of Mary at the Annunciation—when the archangel comes to her suddenly and tells her that she is to bear a child and that child is the Son of God. As theology in paintings goes, it is meant to be symbolic, not of a hunt per se, but of the hunted one, in this instance, the devil having been swallowed up in that moment, without a chance to even wiggle out of the cat's mouth to safety. If you ever see one of these paintings hanging in a museum, imagine a mouse in the belly of that satisfied-looking cat. Imagine the devil's tail hanging out of the cat's mouth at the Annunciation. To pounce is the cat's identity and purpose, their very joy.

Our cats teach us to find our joy and then live it consistently—also one of the essential messages of the Hasidic master Rebbe Nachman of Breslov. Breslov is in what is now Bratslav, Ukraine. Rebbe Nachman is one of the most quoted of the Hasidic rabbis. He was born in the 1770s and died in 1810. He said: "Nothing is as liberating as joy. It frees the mind and fills it with tranquility." He also said, "Losing hope is like losing your freedom, like losing yourself."

Across religious traditions, our teachers show us how to listen to our intuition for pouncing. Each of us has a pounce that is ours to do, and when we do it, we increase joy in the world.

Carlo Carretto, author of the classic *I, Francis*, recreates the voice of Saint Francis. He has the saint speaking autobiographically at the moment when he realizes the teaching of Jesus's incarnation, and Francis in that realization prepared to turn the world upside down: "Every one of us was lord of the world. Every pauper was rich. Every heart was satiated. Every project was possible. I clambered down from the altar and began to dance, barefoot, on the floor of the Church of Saint Damian. I felt like a clown, crazy with joy and life."

Rebbe Nachman's scribe, Reb Noson, himself a prominent Hasidic rebbe (the Hebrew word for "rabbi") of the early nineteenth century, had another of the most interesting teachings on joy I have discovered. Someone asked him how to be happy when life is full of so many disappointments, and Reb Noson replied, "Borrow the happiness." This isn't a superficial response—Reb Noson knew happiness can come and go, but unlike other things that come and go (wealth, popularity, self-confidence—you fill in the blank), there is a reservoir of happiness inside each of us. Perhaps even in the universe. Each of us can remember a time when we were happy, and we can borrow from that reservoir. *Go there, to that place, or to that earlier experience, and get some*, you can still hear Reb Noson saying.

In most everything I see my cats do, I see that deep reservoir of joy. It's become contagious in our home. I think their joy is their experience, but it is also there like a reservoir for us. Maybe this explains why the humans in our house seem to pick up the cats all day long. We love to have them with us. Their presence—and their ability to be present—are gifts.

As we looked at in chapter 5, it's outrageous for people to call cats selfish. Many years ago, when my eldest child was a small girl, I got her a beagle at the local animal shelter. That beagle was so focused on following the scents in front of his nose that he rarely even looked up. This made for a lousy relationship with humans. It would be silly to call that "selfish," however. That's just who he was.

We misunderstand cats when we think their lives have little to do with our own. Cats are centered and they are present. Martin looks at me with eyes that are calm and inviting, even if he doesn't want me to hold him, but his eyes and his posture say we are here together. They are also endowed with physical traits, making their pouncing—their extraordinary balance and movement—beautiful. We humans may not have the balance of a cat, but we are also resilient and surer-footed than we sometimes think. After many pages of analyzing the uniqueness of cheetahs, one of the big cats, zoologist and filmmaker Jackie Higgins concludes:

> We tend to notice our sense of balance only when things go wrong—when we end up . . . sprawled on the floor. It works tirelessly and without conscious perception. It is one of our many secret senses. . . . We know that 100,000 years ago, or thereabouts, it enabled the evolution of the most sure- and fleet-footed animal on earth. Millions of years earlier still, it raised our ancestors from the ground and set them on the path to becoming human.

Be catlike. Trust your own secret sense.

Balancing ourselves to pounce is not limited to those times when they, or we, can see perfectly clearly. We hobble ourselves when we feel we cannot move decisively, or in play, carefreely, without seeing what will happen next. We will never see the future, which doesn't even really exist. Even in the dark, where cats cannot see as well as legend would have it, they move about with no more fear than they have in the light. In both light and darkness, we live fully when we are comfortable with shadows and with glimmers.

Shams of Tabriz, who was the teacher of Jalāl ad-Dīn Muhammad Rūmī, the great twelfth-century Persian Sufi poet, once asked, "Every human being is a 'Word of God'— which 'word' are you?" I think this can be expanded from every human being to every creation. Each is a word of God in some unique way. That is their pounce.

Where is your pounce? Have you been denying it, or are you allowing it to move you? One thing that every cat's human will know is that, if a cat is comfortable with you— and any cat who is cared for is usually comfortable (unless they have been harmed by a previous human or they are in pain)—they will often greet you by lying on their back and looking up into your eyes. They do this to show you they feel safe and protected and as an invitation to you to "pounce" or engage with them. This is their joy. Each day I am trying to return to that experience and to locate the reservoir of joy in myself for the world around me, a lesson the cats continue to teach me.

Practicing What Cats Do Best

I am going to invite you to a spiritual practice that is an imitation of cat behavior. (Similar to chapter 2, where we practiced purring.)

If possible, lay on the floor today. Roll slowly onto your back. Look up. Rock gently from side to side. Keep looking up. Smile.

Or try this: Spend several minutes with the word "pounce." See what happens when you pray, or when you sit in your regular meditation, when you replace a word that is often on your lips or in your heart with "pounce." Be playful with this. For example, if your meditation is scripture, the text you read might become more . . . pounce-y: "Be quiet and know that I am God" (Psalm 46:10) may become "Find your still center of the pounce and know that I am God." Give it a try. See what jumps in you.

Caution and Promise

It has not escaped me that my cats may also be teaching me, or reinforcing in me, habits that are not always good. For example, they like it when I do the same things every day, which means they do not encourage me to be creative or expansive.

There is nothing Rosa wants more than to find me in the same chair every midmorning when she is ready for attention. And there is nothing Martin desires more than to find his breakfast in his bowl at 7:00 a.m. sharp, followed by our bedroom door opening at 7:15 so that he can hop onto the bed and say hello to my wife. And then an hour or so after that, if and when I am at my desk and not paying attention to him at least half-heartedly, he knows exactly where to jump onto the bookcases behind my chair to knock certain objects onto the floor.

My personality works naturally with cats. There are personality reasons why we get along so well. I'm faithful to my routines and find meaning in them. But I don't want to assign virtue to routines such as timekeeping, punctuality, and faithful attention to regular meals. This would be like praising the virtues of an angry hermit simply because he keeps to his prayers, readings, and meals with faithful punctuality. There is no virtue in prayer and contemplation if they don't create in me a better person. The great second surah of the Qur'an speaks to this beautifully when it says: "It is not piety to turn your faces toward the east and west. Rather, piety is he who believes in God, the Last Day, the angels, the Book, and the prophets; and who gives wealth, despite loving it, to kinsfolk, orphans, the indigent, the traveler, beggars, and for [the ransom of] slaves . . . and those who are patient in misfortune, hardship, and moments of peril. It is they who are the sincere, and it is they who are the reverent."

So I have to be careful not to laud my cat qualities and not to allow my cats to keep me from growing and changing toward the good.

I will give you one more example. Just the other morning, my daughter messed up the covers on the spare bed in our house. She was goofing around in the room and left the bed in a rumpled state. I noticed this an hour or so later and didn't think much of it. But then a few hours after that, I caught Martin spraying on the messed-up bed. I was shocked—I thought he'd stopped doing that almost a year ago. But then I was not surprised when I thought more about it. He likes things to be just as they are supposed to be, which means, just as they have always been. That bed is the one bed in our house that, unless someone is visiting, is always neatly made. Both cats like to sit or sleep on it during the day. Martin's serenity had been disturbed. Several hours after discovering the problem, after I had stripped the bed and began washing the sheets and the comforter, there he was settled on the bare mattress looking his usual self, as if the matter had been settled. I'm no cat psychologist, but he looked satisfied, even righteous; I imagine he believed he had done me a favor in pointing out a problem.

So I need more than what I learn from my cats. I also need to be constantly embracing what is new, what is changing, and what needs changing.

I suppose the trick is combining these two things into one life. To combine the discipline necessary to build a real life of spiritual practice and do that while remaining open to what is new—that's the trick we all have to perform. I wouldn't say that doing both is necessarily catlike, so instead I'll say that I learn from my cats' strengths as well as their weaknesses.

We are a tiny but necessary part to play in a cosmic dance, as Joyce Rupp explains so well:

> As I grew older I lost some of my awareness. . . . I was too focused on a busy life of work and often failed to notice. . . . But eventually I made some startling discoveries—three of them—and they have changed my life forever. The first of these is the amazing revelation that I am made of stardust, that every part and parcel of who I am materially was once a piece of a star shining in the heavens. The second discovery is that the air I breathe is the air that has circled the globe and

been drawn in and out by people, creatures and vegetation in lands and seas far away. But the most astounding discovery . . . is the fact that I am part of a vast and marvelous dance that goes on unceasingly at every moment in the most minute particles of the universe.

Martin and Rosa may be unaware of that cosmic picture, but they are still my teachers. We need all the help we can get.

Sources and Further Reading

There are many source notes at the end of this book, pointing you to the experts, authors, and studies that I have quoted in the chapters. In addition to these, the following works informed me at various stages of writing. I recommend them all for those who want to go deeper into these matters. I have divided them into two lists. My mind and heart turns more by the philosophical and contemplative than the inspirational, so the first list represents those that informed my writing most of all.

Philosophical and Contemplative

Coccia, Emanuele. *Metamorphoses*, translated by Robin Mackay. Medford, MA: Polity Press, 2021.

Gray, John. *Feline Philosophy: Cats and the Meaning of Life*. New York: Farrar, Straus & Giroux, 2021.

———. *The Silence of Animals: On Progress and Other Modern Myths*. New York: Farrar, Straus & Giroux, 2014.

This second list is no less important—and in fact represents books that have reached a much wider audience than my book ever will. For every ten books about dogs that are published, there is perhaps one about a cat or cats. Still, there are many to recommend. They are alphabetically presented below, but the first is by far the most loved and common.

Cat Memoir

Amory, Cleveland. *Compleat Cat*. New York: Black Dog & Leventhal, 1995. This is three international bestselling books by Amory in one lovely hardcover volume: *The Cat Who Came for Christmas*; *The Cat and the Curmudgeon*; and *The Best Cat Ever*. You'll find paperback copies of any of these in any used bookstore in the English-speaking world, but since you're most likely to buy them online anyway, you might as well acquire a volume with all three in one.

Brown, Helen. *Cleo: The Cat Who Mended a Family*. New York: Citadel Press, 2010. One of the most charming in the delightful category of human–cat memoir.

Myron, Vicki, with Bret Witter. *Dewey: The Small-Town Library Cat Who Touched the World*. New York: Grand Central Publishing, 2010. As a kitten, Dewey was left, unwanted, in the returned books slot of a public library in Iowa. She was discovered by the author of this memoir, the library's director, who needed Dewey as much as Dewey needed her.

Cat Psychology, Care, and Behavior

Budiansky, Stephen. *The Character of Cats: The Origins, Intelligence, Behavior, and Stratagems of Felis silvestris catus*. New York: Viking, 2002. This is one of the best of cat pop psychology. Even includes a cat personality test.

Janik, Carolyn, and Ruth Rejnis. *The Complete Idiot's Guide to Living with a Cat*. New York: Alpha Books, 1996. Comprehensive work on cat behavior, personalities, and care.

Morris, Desmond. *Catwatching and Catlore: New Enlarged Edition*. London: Arrow Books, 1992. A classic, answering frequent questions such as why cats purr, why cats like being stroked, and why cats prefer to die alone.

Spadafori, Gina, Lauren Demos, and Paul D. Pion. *Cats for Dummies: 3rd Edition*. Hoboken, NJ: John Wiley & Sons, 2020. Up-to-date reference work answering all basic questions for new and experienced cat owners.

Thomas, Elizabeth Marshall. *The Tribe of Tiger: Cats and Their Culture*, illustrated by Jared Taylor Williams. New York: Simon & Schuster, 1994. For those inclined to ponder the big wild cat origins of house cat pets, this is a good place to start.

Cats and Beauty

Surman, Richard. *Cloister Cats*. London: Collins, 2007. Photographs and stories of cats resident at nineteen friaries, monasteries, and abbeys—Anglican, Roman Catholic, and Buddhist—throughout the British Isles and Ireland. The quote from this book in chapter 3 is from page 20.

Cat Stories

There are many books in this rich category. Many of our greatest writers over the last couple of centuries have delighted in writing stories about felines. These are two collections that I've most enjoyed, and I recommend both to you because they do not overlap with each other in their contents.

Brown, Becky, ed. *Classic Cat Stories*. London: Macmillan Collector's Library, 2020.

Robinson, Suzy, ed. *On Cats: An Anthology*. Kendal, UK: Notting Hill Editions, 2021. This book includes an introduction by Margaret Atwood.

About the Author

Jon M. Sweeney is an award-winning author who has been interviewed in print by a range of publications from the *Dallas Morning News* to *The Irish Catholic*, and on television for CBS Saturday Morning and many other programs.

His book, *The Pope Who Quit*, was optioned by HBO. He is also the author of forty other books, including the biographies *Nicholas Black Elk: Medicine Man, Catechist, Saint* and *James Martin, SJ: In the Company of Jesus*; coauthor (with Mark S. Burrows) of *Meister Eckhart's Book of the Heart*, which has been translated and published in other languages; and *Thomas Merton: An Introduction to His Life and Practices*, from St. Martin's Press and Penguin Random House Audio. Jon is also a recognized authority on the life and spirituality of Francis of Assisi and is the author of *The Complete Francis of Assisi* and *Feed the Wolf: Befriending Our Fears in the Way of St. Francis*. And he's the author of the five-volume *The Pope's Cat* series of books for children.

In the late 1990s, Jon cofounded a multifaith publishing house, SkyLight Paths Publishing, in Vermont. Today, he still works in books, speaks regularly at literary and religious conferences, is a Catholic married to Rabbi Michal Woll, and their interfaith marriage has been profiled in national media. He is active on social media (Twitter @jonmsweeney; Facebook jonmsweeney) and lives in Milwaukee with Michal, Sima, Martin, and Rosa (as well as the still thriving goldfish and gerbils).

Acknowledgments

This book began with an e-course sponsored by my friends at Spirituality & Practice (spiritualityandpractice. com) in January 2021. I express my thanks to the hundred or so people who registered for that first dive into what we simply called "The Spirituality of Cats." Our conversations helped deepen my understanding. Thank you also to Frederic and Mary Ann Brussat, founders and codirectors of Spirituality & Practice, with whom I have shared twenty-five years of stories about and love for our felines.

Thank you to Emily McFarlan Miller, correspondent for Religion News Service and another cat lover, for the clever story she wrote about our effort, "New e-course teaches: Copy cats and achieve purrvana."

Agent Joe Durepos was helpful in turning the e-course into a book idea, and Lil Copan at Broadleaf was an enthusiast from the start. My thanks go to both of them, as well.

My son Joe helped me by sharing stories of his early childhood experiences with his cat, Mia, some of which I either had not remembered or hadn't observed.

Notes

Preface

John Gray, *Feline Philosophy: Cats and the Meaning of Life* (New York: Farrar, Straus & Giroux, 2021), 6.

Chapter 1

Atheist becoming a chaplain. See Vanessa Zoltan, *Praying with Jane Eyre: Reflections on Reading as a Spiritual Practice* (New York: TarcherPerigee, 2021).

Ronald Rolheiser, "The Domestic and the Monastic," Column, January 27, 2008, https://ronrolheiser.com/the -domestic-and-the-monastic/#.YdyoWljMITU.

Hafiz. This is my paraphrase, but you will find variants of the same wherever the Sufi mystic's teachings are summarized. For example, see Sadhu T. L. Vaswani, *Sufi Saints of East and West* (New York: Sterling Publishers, 2002), 14.

Abraham Joshua Heschel, *God in Search of Man: A Philosophy of Judaism* (New York: Farrar Straus & Giroux, 1976), 404.

Cynthia Bourgeault, *Eye of the Heart: A Spiritual Journey into the Imaginal Realm* (Boulder, CO: Shambhala, 2020), 81.

Chapter 2

Behavioral Processes. Both journal studies are mentioned in a *New York Times* article from 2019: Rachel Nuwer, "Cats Like People (Some People, Anyway)," *New York Times*, September 24, 2019, https://www.nytimes.com/2019/09/24/science/cats-humans-bonding.html#:~:text=In%20a%202019%20study%2C%20the,that%20cats%20know%20their%20names.

Suzy Robinson, ed., *On Cats: An Anthology* (Kendal, UK: Notting Hill Editions, 2021), 89.

Purring in nursing kittens. Desmond Morris, *Catwatching and Catlore: New Enlarged Edition* (London: Arrow Books, 1992), 15.

Thich Nhat Hanh, *The Pocket Thich Nhat Hanh*, ed. Melvin McLeod (Boston: Shambhala, 2012), 138.

Pierre Teilhard de Chardin, *Human Energy*, trans. J. M. Cohen (New York: Harcourt Brace Jovanovich: 1969), 32.

Mary Oliver, ed., "On the Beach," in *Devotions: The Selected Poems of Mary Oliver* (New York: Penguin Press, 2017), 65.

Chapter 3

Bernard of Clairvaux letter to Robert, in Caroline Walker Bynum, *Jesus as Mother: Studies in the Spirituality of the High Middle Ages* (Berkeley: University of California Press, 1984), 116–17. I have adapted the translation slightly.

Kenneth L. Woodward, "'Lived from the Heart' an Interview with Bernard McGinn," *Commonweal*, January 2022, 37.

Francis of Assisi, on being like mothers, *The Complete Francis of Assisi*, ed. and trans. Jon M. Sweeney (Brewster, MA: Paraclete Press, 2015), 231.

Psalm 16:11, NRSV.

Diana L. Eck, *Darsan: Seeing the Divine Image in India, Third Edition* (New York: Columbia University Press, 1998), 3.

Replacing mother cat: Desmond Morris, *Catwatching and Catlore*, 39. Feral cats pooping in a prominent place: Desmond Morris, *Catwatching and Catlore*, 81.

Chapter 4

Cats responsible for death of songbirds: See data of the American Bird Conservancy: https://abcbirds.org/program/cats-indoors/cats-and-birds/.

Edwin F. Bryant, translated with introduction and notes. *Krishna: The Beautiful Legend of God: (Srimad Bhagavata Purana Book X)* (New York: Penguin Books, 2003).

John Grimes, *A Concise Dictionary of Indian Philosophy: Sanskrit Terms Defined in English, New and Revised Edition* (Albany: State University of New York Press, 1996).

Simon Gathercole, trans., "The Infancy Gospel of Thomas," in *The Apocryphal Gospels* (London: Penguin Books, 2021), 31–32.

See Iris Murdoch's novel, *Henry and Cato* (Glasgow: Triad and Granada, 1983), 154.

Henri Nouwen. See for instance, Michael Ford, *Wounded Prophet: A Portrait of Henri J. M. Nouwen* (New York: Image, 2002).

Christina the Astonishing. See Elizabeth Spearing, ed., *Medieval Writings on Female Spirituality* (New York: Penguin, 2002), 75–86.

Chapter 5

John Gray, *Feline Philosophy*, 18.

Baal Shem Tov. Martin Buber, *Tales of the Hasidim: The Early Masters*, trans. Olga Marx (New York: Schocken Books, 1947), 45.

Sufi commentator. Al-Nisaburi, as quoted by Kristin Zahra Sands, *Sufi Commentaries on the Qur'an in Classical Islam* (New York: Routledge, 2000), 102.

John the Short. *The Desert Fathers: Sayings of the Early Christian Monks*, trans. Benedicta Ward (New York: Penguin, 2003), 22.

Seyyed Hossein Nasr, ed., *The Study Quran: A New Translation and Commentary* (New York: HarperOne, 2015), 79. And for the alternative translation offered, "What Rewards Am I Seeking from Fasting," Blog post, University of Manchester Islamic Society, https://www.manchesterisoc.com/blog/what-rewards-am-i-seeking-from-fasting/.

Chapter 6

Ecclesiastes 4:11–12, NIV.

Hildegard of Bingen, in *Original Blessings: A Primer in Creation Spirituality*, trans. Matthew Fox (Santa Fe, NM: Bear & Company, 1983), 184.

Teresa of Avila, from *Teresa of Avila: Mystical Writings*, trans. Tessa Bielecki (New York: Crossroad Publishing, 1997), 41.

Malcolm X, letter, written August 25, 1964, can be read in facsimile online at various websites including here: https://www.dailymail.co.uk/news/article-3277981/Letter-written-Malcolm-X-sale-1-25-million.html.

Charles Flood, SCJ, *The Lakota Prayer Book: Inspiration for Daily Life* (Chamberlain, SD: St. Joseph's Indian School, 1992), 12.

Chapter 7

Cleveland Amory, *The Cat Who Came for Christmas* (New York: Back Bay Books, 2013).

Wisława Szymborska, *Nobel Lectures: From the Literature Laureates, 1986 to 2006* (New York: The New Press, 2008). Also available on-line at https://www.nobelprize.org/prizes/literature/1996/szymborska/lecture/.

Recent study of cat attachment behavior. Kristyn R. Vitale, Alexandra C. Behnke, and Monique A. R. Udell, "Attachment Bonds between Domestic Cats and Human," *Current Biology* 29 (September 23, 2019); see figure 1 on R865.

Nuns of the Bus: https://networklobby.org/nunsonthebus/.

Daniel Berrigan and Robert Coles, *The Geography of Faith: Underground Conversations on Religious, Political, and Social Change* (Woodstock, VT: SkyLight Paths, 2001), 36.

Sr. Simone Campbell, *Hunger for Hope: Prophetic Communities, Contemplation, and the Common Good* (Maryknoll, NY: Orbis Books, 2020), 127.

Chapter 8

Saint Teresa of Avila, from *The Way of Perfection*, in *The Collected Works of Saint Teresa of Avila, Volume Two*, trans. Kieran Kavanaugh, OCD and Otilio Rodriguez, OCD (Washington, DC: ICS Publications, 1980), 107.

John Sullivan, OCD, ed., *Edith Stein: Essential Writings* (Maryknoll, NY: Orbis Books, 2002), 64.

Christine Valters Paintner, AbbeyoftheHearts.com, https://abbeyofthearts.com/blog/2011/08/25/the-transforming-power-of-lectio-divina-a-deeper-look-at-the-four-movements/.

Paul Quenon, OCSO, *Amounting to Nothing: Poems* (Brewster, MA: Paraclete Press, 2019).

Chapter 9

Sister Annabel Laity, ed., *Thich Nhat Hanh: Essential Writings* (Maryknoll, NY: Orbis Books, 2001), 122.

Seyyed Hossein Nasr, ed., *The Study Quran: A New Translation and Commentary* (New York: HarperOne, 2015), 19: 93–96; 786.

Bonnie Myotai Treace, *Wake Up: How to Practice Zen Buddhism* (Emeryville, CA: Rockridge Press, 2019), x–xi.

Chapter 10

Lydia Davis, *The Cows* (Louisville, KY: Sarabande Books, 2011), 11–12.

John Gray, *Feline Philosophy*, 110.

Anne Lamott, *Help Thanks Wow: The Three Essential Prayers* (New York: Riverhead, 2012).

Brother David Steindl-Rast, Gratefulness.org, https://gratefulness.org/resource/what-is-gratitude/.

Chapter 11

Michel de Montaigne, *The Essays of Montaigne: Volume 1*, trans. E. J. Trechmann (London: Oxford University Press, 1927), from "Apology for Raimond Sebond," 441, 444.

Alexandra Sellers, *How to Speak Cat: The Essential Primer of Cat Language* (New York: Harper Collins, 1998), 5.

"The Questions of Bartholomew," in *The Apocryphal Gospels*, trans. Simon Gathercole (New York: Penguin, 2021), 289–90.

Chapter 12

Grimms' fairy tale, "Cat and Mouse in Partnership": Joseph Campbell and Padraic Colum, eds., *The Complete Grimm's Fairy Tales* (New York: Pantheon Books, 1972), 23.

Displacement activities: The Cats International website has a good article on this, as they do on many topics. https://catsinternational.org/displacement-activities-and -stereotypes/.

Enneagram Eight and Enneagram Nine: Ian Morgan Cron, *The Story of You: An Enneagram Journey to Becoming Your True Self* (New York: HarperOne, 2021), 35, 55.

Chapter 13

Oscar the nursing home cat: David M. Dosa, "A Day in the Life of Oscar the Cat," *The New England Journal of Medicine* (July 2007), https://www.nejm.org/doi/full/10.1056/NEJMp078108.

Oncologists writing on cats: David P. Steenma, "The Scent of Cancer," *Annals of Internal Medicine* (August 2010), https://www.acpjournals.org/doi/abs/10.7326/0003-4819-153-3-201008030-00014?journalCode=aim.

Thich Nhat Hanh, *Path of Compassion: Stories from the Buddha's Life* (Berkeley, CA: Parallax Press, 2008), 72.

Wendell Berry, *This Day: Sabbath Poems Collected and New, 1979–2013* (Berkeley, CA: Counterpoint, 2013), 7.

Mary Oliver, *Devotion: The Selected Poems of Mary Oliver* (New York: Penguin, 2020), 107–8.

Annie Dillard, *Pilgrim at Tinker Creek* (New York: Harper Perennial, 2013), 16.

Chapter 14

Joy Harjo, *Poet Warrior: A Memoir* (New York: W. W. Norton, 2021), 186.

Cats listening to us on the phone. Desmond Morris, *Catwatching and Catlore*, 29.

Paul Zak, "Dogs (and Cats) Can Love," *The Atlantic*, April 22, 2014, https://www.theatlantic.com/health/archive/2014/04/does-your-dog-or-cat-actually-love-you/360784/.

Desmond Tutu, from an NPR interview: Frederic Brussat and Mary Ann Brussat, *Spiritual Literacy: Reading the Sacred in Everyday Life* (New York: Scribner, 1998), 275.

Chapter 15

Samuel L. Perry, "How Religion Predicts Pet Ownership in the United States," *Journal for the Scientific Study of Religion* 59, no. 1 (March 2020). I'm quoting from the excerpt, and my reaction to it that was published in *The Tablet* for January 10, 2020. thetablet.co.uk.

John G. Neihardt, *Black Elk Speaks: Being the Story of a Holy Man of the Oglala Sioux* (Albany, NY: State University of New York Press, 2008), 307.

John Gray, *Feline Philosophy*, 110.

Julian of Norwich, from her *Showings*. Repeated verbatim by T. S. Eliot in "Little Gidding," the last part of his *Four Quartets*.

Meister Eckhart, from "On Detachment," in *Treatises and Sermons of Meister Eckhart*, trans. James M. Clark and John V. Skinner (New York: Harper & Brothers, 1958), 167–68. I have altered the translation in several places.

See the Jewish morning blessings in *Kol Haneshamah: Shabbat Vegahim* (Elkins Park, PA: The Reconstructionist Press, 1994), 152–61. This is the weekly prayer book of the Reconstructing Judaism movement.

Chapter 16

Alexandra Sellers, *How to Speak Cat: The Essential Primer of Cat Language* (New York: Harper Collins, 1998), xvi.

The UK study description is quoted from *Tigers: The World's Most Extraordinary Animals* (New York: Life/Meredith Corporation, 2021), 82.

Obedience and knowledge in the Hebrew scriptures. See for instance, Hosea 4:1 in the New Revised Standard Version ("Hear the word of the Lord, O people of Israel. . . . There is no faithfulness or loyalty, and no knowledge of God in the land.") vs. in the *JPS Hebrew-English Tanakh* ("Hear the word of the Lord, O people of Israel! . . . Because there is no honesty and no goodness and no obedience to God in the land.").

Willa Blythe Baker, *The Wakeful Body: Somatic Mindfulness as a Path to Freedom* (Boulder, CO: Shambhala, 2021), 107.

Chapter 17

Candice Lin, "Seeping, Rotting, Resting, Weeping," Walker Art Center, Minneapolis, MN, 2021. Also, interview with Candice Lin in *ArtForum* (November 1, 2021), https://www.artforum.com/interviews/candice-lin-on -collective-grief-and-the-consolation-of-cats-86884.

Ursula LeGuin, in Suzy Robinson, *On Cats*, 90.

Rebbe Nachman of Breslov and Reb Noson: See the many resources of the Breslov Research Institute in Jerusalem, including this page on their website: https://breslov.org /borrow-the-happiness/.

Carlo Carretto, *I, Francis*, trans. Robert R. Barr (Maryknoll, NY: Orbis Books, 1982), 15.

Jackie Higgins, *Sentient: How Animals Illuminate the Wonder of Our Human Senses* (New York: Atria Books, 2022), 182–83.

Shams of Tabriz, quoted by Camille Hamilton Adams Helminski, *The Way of Mary: Maryam, Beloved of God* (Louisville, KY: Sweet Lady Press, 2021), 86.

Conclusion

Quotation from the second surah. Seyyed Hossein Nasr, ed., *The Study Quran: A New Translation and Commentary* (New York: HarperOne, 2015), 2:177.

Commentary on piety in 2:177: *The Study Quran*, 75–76.

Michael Leach, ed., *Joyce Rupp: Essential Writings* (Maryknoll, NY: Orbis Books, 2017), 118–19.